# LIFE *in the* SPIRIT WORLD

Communicated to Medium
**Muriel Williams**

By the late Professor
**Ian Currie**

Research and Narration
**Bill Williams,** *Ph.D.*

© Copyright 2006 Bill Williams
All rights reserved. No part of this publication may be reproduced, stored in a retrieval system, or transmitted, in any form or by any means, electronic, mechanical, photocopying, recording, or otherwise, without the written prior permission of the author.

Note for Librarians: A cataloguing record for this book is available from Library and Archives Canada at www.collectionscanada.ca/amicus/index-e.html
ISBN 1-55369-098-2

*Offices in Canada, USA, Ireland and UK*

This book was published *on-demand* in cooperation with Trafford Publishing. On-demand publishing is a unique process and service of making a book available for retail sale to the public taking advantage of on-demand manufacturing and Internet marketing. On-demand publishing includes promotions, retail sales, manufacturing, order fulfilment, accounting and collecting royalties on behalf of the author.

**Book sales for North America and international:**
Trafford Publishing, 6E–2333 Government St.,
Victoria, BC V8T 4P4 CANADA
phone 250 383 6864 (toll-free 1 888 232 4444)
fax 250 383 6804; email to orders@trafford.com

**Book sales in Europe:**
Trafford Publishing (UK) Limited, 9 Park End Street, 2nd Floor
Oxford, UK OX1 1HH UNITED KINGDOM
phone 44 (0)1865 722 113 (local rate 0845 230 9601)
facsimile 44 (0)1865 722 868; info.uk@trafford.com

**Order online at:**
trafford.com/01-0500

10 9 8 7 6 5 4 3 2

## Professor Ian Currie's Mission Statement

"We conclude here without a doubt that there is life after death, based on the many incarnations we went through and how we render a service to mankind on the earth planet. From searching my previous lifetimes I tried to do this before by teaching from spirit through a medium in Britain. This was a couple of lifetimes ago in the late eighteenth century. I then returned to this last one where I again absorbed myself in the paranormal. There is a definite pattern in our lifetimes. Now, once again I need to finish this era by getting this book out to the people of planet earth, proving to human beings – there is continuous life. This is the essence of the whole book."

Dedicated to the memory of

**Muriel Williams
1926 – 2003**

*"Trusting that, through this book,
your light will shine brightly on your spiritual path."*
– Muriel Williams

# Acknowledgements

My deepest respect and gratitude go to my dear wife Muriel who worked with great dedication to make this book happen. Her wonderful gift of mediumship gave her the ability to communicate with those who had passed to spirit life. This book was an opportunity for her to share that gift with others; it is now her legacy and a wish fulfilled.

My thanks go to Tricia whose love, support and creative contributions were an integral part of this book. I am also grateful to my daughter Cherie for her patience and diligence in completing the editing process. She picked up the baton shortly after Muriel's passing, and ran the last mile, or maybe it was miles, to the finishing line.

Thanks go also to our nephew Kevin McCall who was responsible for designing the book cover, and to Max Izod for his expertise in print and layout.

The completion of this project was not plain sailing and there were many obstacles to surmount in the process. However commitment and a true belief in the validity of the content of this book were the driving forces, which brought it to fruition.

Bill Williams

# Contents

| | | |
|---|---|---|
| Acknowledgements | | vii |
| Editorial Preface | | xi |
| Introduction | | xiv |
| Chapter 1 | **First Contact** | 1 |
| | Professor Currie Makes his Entrance – Establishing Rapport – Reflection | |
| Chapter 2 | **Crossing the Veil** | 9 |
| | The Professor describes his Passing | |
| | Research Notes: Spirit Visitations and the Process of Dying | |
| Chapter 3 | **Adjusting to Spirit Life** | 17 |
| | Ian describes his Surroundings – Setting up Office – Colour | |
| | Research Notes: Colour | |
| Chapter 4 | **Spirit Lifestyle** | 23 |
| | Music – Spirit Time – Levels of Friendship – Energy breaks during Communication – Emanuel Swedenborg – Spirit Travel – Trips to Universities | |
| | Research Notes: Alcohol in the Spirit World; Brief Historical Note on Emanuel Swedenborg/Swedberg; Professor Baird | |
| Chapter 5 | **Energy and Light** | 37 |
| | Communicating with Spirit – Life with a Capital 'L' – Centre of Energy – Turquoise Light | |
| | Research Notes: Psychic Light; Energy | |
| Chapter 6 | **Teaching in Spirit** | 49 |
| | Professor Currie Teaches in the Spirit World – Awareness Therapy – The Professor meets Young Souls – You are your Soul | |
| Chapter 7 | **Masters and Guides** | 59 |
| | Inauguration of a Philosopher – Guides – Healing Guides – Ian's Guides – Masters | |
| Chapter 8 | **Reincarnation** | 69 |
| | Choosing Parents – Conception and the Soul – Children in Spirit – Pets in the Spirit World | |
| | Research Notes: Pets | |

| Chapter 9 | **Spirit Communication** | 81 |

Psychics and Spirit Contact – Information from my Level –
  Spirit Impostors and Poltergeists – New Challenges in the World
Research Notes: Poltergeists; Spirit Impostors

| Chapter 10 | **Untimely Departures** | 95 |

Suicide – Euthanasia – Murder
Research Notes: Euthanasia, DNR and Suicide

| Chapter 11 | **Out-of-Body Experiences** | 103 |

What is an Out-of-Body Experience? –
  Near-Death Experiences – Dreams

| Chapter 12 | **The Mind and its Mysteries** | 111 |

The Mind – Memory – Personality – Multiple Personalities –
  Possession – The Blue Planet
Research Notes: Multiple Personalities and Possession;
  The Blue Planet and the Blue Island

| Chapter 13 | **Spirituality and Religion** | 125 |

Religion – Spiritual Planes – Understanding Spirit – Fate –
  Celebrations in the Spirit World – Christmas –
  Free Will – Repentance and Renewal

| Chapter 14 | **Levels and Planes** | 137 |

Spiritual Progress – The Lower Levels – Akashic Records –
  Soul Progress
Research Notes: Soul Progression

| Chapter 15 | **Final Thoughts from Ian Currie** | 149 |

| Epilogue | **The Survival of Intelligence and Personality** | 155 |

| Bibliographic References | | 187 |

| Appendices | **Appendix I** | 191 |

An autobiographical account of the mediumship of Muriel Williams

**Appendix II**  201

A sample of Muriel's handwritten notes of the conversations

| Index | | 205 |

# Editorial Preface

The conversations reproduced in this book are purportedly from the spirit of the late Professor Ian Currie, through the psychic gifts of Muriel Williams. I do not know the views of those of you who will be reading this book: you may just be curious or interested in the subject matter; you may be a firm believer; or you may be a sceptic. You may find it strange that the apparent "appearances" and conversations of Professor Currie are so easily accepted by the authors of this book. You may have known Professor Ian Currie, or you may not. I did not know him, his academic work, or his work on the paranormal before reading an earlier draft of this book. Whatever you think, whoever you think the spirit is (even if you believe there is a spirit communication at all), you will still find a message of great love and hope for the world.

If you are a reader who was privileged to have known Ian Currie either professionally or personally, I hope you will find that we have treated his memory, through these conversations, with respect and care. I hope you will understand that there is no intention to undermine his life, nor should there be any sense of disservice to his life, nor is there any lack of respect for him, his life or his work. What comes across here is a person of great warmth and humour.

Through the messages and conversations the reader will discover someone who appears to have an incredible knowledge of the afterlife, who wanted to be able to communicate about it, and who had the drive and energy to seek to find out more about subjects about which he was unsure. You will also discover an intelligent man who had the humility to correct any of his views if he subsequently discovered that they were incorrect or unclear. He also seems to be someone who enjoyed his earth life and had a real sense of humour. It is also clear, from his personal remarks and jokes about Bill and Muriel Williams that he knew them both very well! His comments and appreciation of Muriel also meant that he was sure about her mediumistic gifts.

Those of you, like me, who did not know Ian Currie, may only ever know the professor through this book (or maybe you, like me, will be prompted to read his book now). Those of you who did know him will make your own judgement about the source of these conversations, but it is absolutely clear from the conversations and descriptions that both Muriel and Bill Williams believe that they are the words of Professor Ian Currie.

The exact source of these conversations may not be important for some of you at all: you may only be concerned with the content. Others of you may have wanted more "proof" of the authorship. Whatever your position, I am sure you will agree that the words in this book give incredible food for thought. Some parts of the book may help in the preparation for what is to come; other parts may confirm existing views. Nothing is claimed here, for nothing can be claimed. I can only hope that this particular insight into life in the spirit world will ease your load in life.

It has been a privilege and a great journey of learning for me to be involved in the final stages of the publication of this book. After Muriel's illness and her passing to the spirit world it was hard for both Bill and Tricia to continue with the work that had been such an important part in the lives of the three of them. I therefore took on the role of editor in order to prepare the draft manuscript for publication. However the final message and work that you have before you is the product of the partnership between Bill, Ian, Muriel and Tricia. My involvement served only to open up a new path in my own life and thereby lessen my burden – I hope it can ease your load in life too.

Cherie Knowles D'Silva, Ph.D
Leicester, UK

# Introduction

Before anyone begins to read these communications from the spirit of the late Professor Ian Currie, it is only fitting to know just how Muriel and Bill came to know the professor when he was alive; also how their paths in life were guided to the creation of this most revealing book.

It was in the spring of 1985 when Bill Williams first met the professor, who was one of the key lecturers at the Association for Past Life Experiences. Their contact continued on a professional and personal basis, which led subsequently to his introduction to Muriel. He would consult with her from time to time for psychic guidance on private matters and all three learnt much from each other as both colleagues and friends.

Sometime later Ian's health started to deteriorate, with recurring bouts of illness. On one of the occasions of his return from hospital, he asked Bill to see him at his home. Bill spent many days during Ian's initial convalescence sorting out his business affairs. It was during this time, while walking in High Park, Toronto that a pact was made between them, stating whoever passed away first would endeavour to make contact through a psychic or a medium.

Sadly Bill's friend passed to spirit on the 5th July 1992. One month to the day later, on the 5th August 1992, the spirit of Professor Ian Currie made his first appearance to Muriel, communicating from the spirit world on the subway train at Finch Station, Toronto. These communications continued over a period of years and built up to over a hundred conversations; they have culminated in the amazing explanations and detailed descriptions in this book.

*Life in the Spirit World*' embraces the expertise of three main parties who found that their paths had been guided towards the creation of this work: the spirit of the late Professor Ian Currie – the communicator, Muriel Williams – the medium, and Bill Williams – the researcher and narrator. Besides the research and narration, it was also Bill's task to prepare the pertinent questions for the professor to answer. They were also supported throughout this work by Muriel's cousin and lifelong friend, Tricia Cochran, who was to become a competent healer with her own developing psychic abilities.

## Ian Currie – the Communicator

The late Professor Ian Currie, through his communication from the realm of spirit, and at his request, provided the extensive subject matter for this book. The professor, who was born in Vancouver, Canada, studied for his sociology doctorate at the University of California, USA, and later he became Professor of Sociology at Toronto University. For much of his life, however, his main interests were parapsychology and psychical research.

Ian Currie collaborated with colleagues from a wide range of disciplines to teach courses on death and dying. His best known book *'You Cannot Die'* was first published in 1978 and quickly raced to the best seller list in several countries. Ian Currie continued to investigate the mysteries of life after death through his practice of past life therapy (with over 4000 regressions) and through the exorcism of nuisance ghosts. At the age of 56 he had already prepared material for future books but, unfortunately, he was prematurely taken from us after some surgical complications before these works could be published.

## Muriel Williams – the Medium

Muriel Williams was the medium through whom the late Professor Ian Currie purportedly communicated directly from spirit. Muriel was born Muriel Mary McDonald Davidson, in Aberdeen, Scotland in 1926. The visions and voices she saw from the age of eight in the fields of her father's small farm were the beginnings of the development of her gifts as a clairvoyant, clairaudient and clairsentient psychic: she was a rare *tripartite medium*. While following a career in the Performing Arts as a professional singer and dancer in London, England, she studied mediumship at the Spiritualist Association of Great Britain[1], and was a member of that association.

After settling in Toronto, Canada in 1979 Muriel continued to give spiritual guidance to those in need while pursuing a business career. She had just begun to pursue and develop her psychic gifts on a full-time basis when, too soon for all those who knew her, Muriel became seriously ill in the summer of 2002 and was taken into the spirit world in January 2003. She was so sad that she was not able to finish the book before her passing – but there is no doubt that she is still guiding the

---

[1] In those days it was known as The Marylebone Spiritualist Association (MSA).

book through to its completion.

## Bill Williams – the Researcher and Narrator

It was the pioneering spirit and enquiring mind of Bill Williams which made him leave his birthplace in India before that country gained its independence. He settled in London, England in 1948 with his family and began a varied career which included acting and politics. Later he met Muriel and, from 1963, he began his research into metaphysics and the paranormal. Bill became a member of the College of Psychic Studies, attending many seminars, demonstrations and courses on psychic phenomena. He also became involved in developing circles for those with psychic gifts.

In 1979, with Muriel and Tricia, he left the UK to settle in Toronto, Canada and set up a new business. However his paranormal research was never far from his mind and he continued to pursue his path and give lectures on his psychic interests. Through the Association for Past Life Experiences he met Ian Currie and many of his colleagues and, from this, instituted and established an annual lecture on 'Life After Death' at the University of Toronto. The first of these took place in March, 1998. Bill Williams has ceaselessly continued to use his unquestionable drive and passion for evidence of life after death to produce the book that is here before you[2].

## The Relationship

Muriel and Tricia were both from Aberdeen in Scotland and became

---

[2] See Epilogue for more information about Bill's undeniable lifelong quest for evidence. Also see www.evidencefromthespirtworld.com

best friends initially through their performance as dancers. They came to describe themselves as 'cousins' – even though they were not blood-related. However from the start of their friendship more than 50 years ago, Tricia was an accepted member of Muriel's family. They both began their careers in the Performing Arts, although Tricia went on to become a costume designer and subsequently a renowned couturier. She has continued to support both Bill and Muriel throughout their lives.

The marriage of Bill and Muriel Williams was a very significant union, because it brought together two people who shared an unshakeable belief in the existence of an Afterlife. Their meeting was not by chance, it came through the endeavours of a mutual friend – a healer who was a member of the Spiritualist Association of Great Britain. In Muriel's own words:

> *"The most influential happening in my life, was meeting my husband Bill. This came about through a healer friend who was part of the M.S.A. healing group and she arranged for Bill and I to meet. He was a part-time actor and I a singer and we shared a common interest in the field of the paranormal."* [3]

All three of them shared the conviction that they had come together to form a 'Spiritual Partnership' in order to learn from each other. They had always worked with the triangle or pyramid as their model i.e. two of them at the base supporting the one at the top – throughout the many years they had spent together on many diverse projects, they had each in turn taken over one of the roles or been equally balanced.

---

[3] See Appendix I for a longer autobiographical note which is the source of this extract.

This book is the culmination of all the work that has gone before – and is the evidence that they have knowledge which they wish to share with others. It is this powerful combination that has resulted in the creation of the book currently being presented. It has taken years of dedication to bring this project to fruition and represents a vision which has finally been realised.

## The Conversations

Muriel has written copious notes[4], which she carefully recorded during her many sessions with the professor. Muriel's conversations with Professor Ian Currie were always done alone except for one communication *'Crossing the Veil'* which was tape-recorded, where Tricia and Bill were also present, and Bill asked the questions directly to Ian. This session was experimental and was not repeated. In many sessions Bill prepared questions for Muriel to ask or the topics were decided by Ian.

The conversations ranged over so many topics each time, with Tricia undertaking the painstaking work of putting the detailed 100+ conversations together into their various headings. It was Muriel who focused her spiritual energy[5] on this work and, despite her natural reluctance to write in normal life, she faithfully made a written recording of the hours and hours of conversation, whilst at the same time ensuring that every one of Bill's questions was asked as accurately as possible, returning to Ian for further clarification when needed. It was Bill who researched the references and general points, always needing more proof. Bill's own mother was a medium and she affectionately called him her "doubting

---

[4] A sample of these notes (all dated and made contemporaneously) can be found in Appendix II.
[5] For a fuller description of how Muriel focused her energies see Chapter 5: Energy and Light.

Thomas" for always wanting more proof. However it was this enquiring and researching mind which has continued through his lifetime to fuel his passion and drive to find substantial proof of life after death. He strongly believes that the conversations detailed in this work provide the evidence to a standard that is incontrovertible.

Despite Bill's belief in the evidence provided by this book, he is also strongly aware how much more needs to be done. As you, the reader, travel through this work, you will find several references to how much more needs to be understood in the Afterlife. Professor Ian Currie refers to topics as being "way out of my league"; or that he "can't confirm – will progress to understanding". He talks of going to "lectures" and the need to "procure and prepare information" to answer the questions. He also often says that he has described his life in the spirit world "as I currently see things" or "from my own perspective and grade of soul energy". Clearly, therefore, the reader has been given information as Ian Currie, from his standpoint and spiritual development, understands it to be.

It is also important to mention here that in the construction of the book, it was necessary in the interest of good reading and also to maintain continuity, to assimilate the information provided by Professor Currie under subject headings. In order to do this successfully, references pertaining to a given subject had to be extracted from the notes and correlated accordingly. Often the Professor would talk on several different topics in one conversation and also might refer back to a topic in a later conversation. It was also very important to maintain the integrity of the text, and keep intact the special rapport that Muriel and the professor enjoyed during their communications. Professor Currie always addressed the subject under discussion with a frankness and candour that was his unique style of delivery. Throughout the book you will notice that some of his words, sentences and phrases have been shown in italics. If he made a statement, which is considered to be important or profound, Bill has taken the liberty of emphasizing the point as being worthy of your attention.

Ian speaks directly to Muriel in his own inimitable style as a Professor, highlighting his unusual spontaneous wit, in relating his personal findings of spirit life. He states in this book that he is 'at home' in the spirit world, and that he continues his previous work on reincarnation, preparing spirit 'students' for further earthly incarnations. At times he would bring students to witness his communication – it is fascinating that he continues this work in his spirit life.

In Chapter 1 Muriel describes her first contact with Ian but it is most pertinent to finish this introduction with Muriel's own words as she recorded them when the conversations had finished.

> *Communicating with Ian has been a privilege and a wonderful experience for me; I now have a full picture of where I'm going to – when my time comes to leave this world. Ian has truly tried to give you his perspective of 'Life Eternal.' I know he will be happy if he reaches you, knowing that you will give it some thought. I will now leave you to enjoy Ian's vision of:*

## Life in the Spirit World

# 1
## First Contact

*"I will communicate again and give you my interpretation of the afterlife. Meantime, tell Bill the good news is – there is one. Life continues."*
– Ian Currie

**Professor Currie makes his Entrance**

**Muriel:** I'm sitting on the subway train on my way to business. The train has just pulled out of the station. I close my eyes and settle into my customary short meditation to connect with my 'spirit mentor' Chung[1]. Suddenly, I am aware Chung has allowed a strong spirit presence to enter my energy field. The vibration brings a sense of urgency and purpose.

I focus on this new energy and the vision of Professor Ian Currie manifests in front of me. I was taken aback by his unexpected appearance and communicated my surprise and pleasure. He smiled and indicated he wished me to write; so I rummaged hurriedly through my bag searching for writing material, still feeling a sense of urgency and not wanting to lose his vibration. I found some paper and as he began to speak, I wrote …

---

[1] See Chapter 5 for a fuller description of how Muriel prepares herself for spirit communication. Additionally the reader may wish to refer to Chapter 7: Masters and Guides.

**Ian:** "The importance of being earnest is much more than words can express. *It is impossible to eliminate the pain of death.* Unfortunately, some have to go through more than others before crossing the veil. In the end all of us come to rest in peace and tranquillity, although this is only the beginning of the next phase in one's journey.

"On recalling my recent attempt at life, – in general I feel I could have made a better job of it. We seek perfection but each soul takes its own time getting there ... many generations later. Sometimes one reaches only a certain level of perfection – not the epitome; but the nearest that can be achieved. Only a few souls qualify for the highest. I mean to bring you as much information as I can. I will communicate again and give you my interpretation of the afterlife. Meantime, tell Bill the good news is – there is one. Life continues!"

**Muriel:** At this point the train was arriving at my subway stop and I had to make a very hasty exit on to the platform – notepaper in hand, bag and all. Being in a slight state of disorientation, I sat down on the nearest bench to collect my thoughts and examine what I had just written. I'm thinking – wow Ian, you could have chosen a more appropriate moment to make your first communication.

However I read over my scribble and felt a thrill of excitement at the prospect of receiving first hand information from the 'spirit world' from a source I knew to be completely reliable: I had seen the spirit of Ian standing in front of me and Chung, my guide and mentor, giving Ian permission to connect directly with me.

I arrived at our place of business and phoned Bill, still excited at what had taken place on my way to work. He realized that Ian, his friend and co-researcher into the afterlife, had kept his promise – that whoever would pass away first would attempt to make contact.

Later that evening Bill, my cousin Tricia, and I discussed the communication. It seemed obvious that Ian meant business and wished to communicate again. We recognized the importance of this work and decided that, to avoid further disquieting moments, it would be beneficial for both parties to have a set time and venue for the communication. This way I could give my full attention to what Ian had to say.

It was the start of many informative, sometimes provocative, and often entertaining conversations – I discovered Ian had a great sense of humour. It is best to establish early that Chung who is the controller of my channel does not allow unwanted entities to make their presence felt. Should I wish to make contact with any spirit entity, permission has to be obtained first before contact is made. Hence, Ian would have to wait for clearance to speak.

**Bill:** Before Muriel was able to set a firm pattern of spirit communication with the professor, she had to establish the correct rapport with him. This turned out to be quite a process in itself, simply because it was a relatively short period from the time of Ian's passing to the time of his first communication with Muriel. Communication with a recently deceased person can sometimes be difficult before a rest period has been completed, although Muriel has had many instances of very early communication from souls just newly passed over, anxious to make contact with loved ones to reassure them that they lived on.

Having said that however, it is reasonable to assume there would necessarily have to be a period of adjustment before any serious in-depth communications could be undertaken. The soul needs time to become familiar with the spiritual environment now called home, and to come to terms with the life just lived. Muriel now discusses how she gradually nurtured Ian into a true spirit of co-operation before engaging him in lengthy conversation.

**Establishing Rapport**

**Muriel:** During the next few months, I would tune in with Ian on my own just to find out how he was coping with living in his new world. To my mind it was the same as calling a friend on the phone just to let him know we were thinking about him. He would tell me he was settling into his new life, and during our conversations would talk about his feelings, and how he really had arrived in spirit prematurely. Of course he was well aware that it was probably his own fault. Sometimes I sensed him to be in a state of depression – a condition that was problematic in his life, and then suddenly, his great sense of humour would shine through and save the day. I promise you will come across these gems as the book unfolds.

The following is a short conversation from the early days, related with Ian's permission.

> **Ian:** "Muriel I feel rather lethargic today, but not to worry we will continue. I was reminiscing and entered into a sad mood and did not really care whether we prove to the world that there is life after death. I know I should not do this but just could not help it. People can do as they please here, because hell, there is

no time frame. One stays with one's own personality until reincarnating to the earth plane. I use the term earth plane, because it is just another plane in the evaluation of progress."

**Muriel:** *"Come on Ian, you have to get to grips with yourself and work at all this. Give us proof, beyond doubt, about eternal life. You are equipped with all the correct thinking to make this happen. You came to me, wanting to do this book, because you had spent most of your lifetime trying to get answers. Now you have first hand information, and can provide answers to many questions. You told me a few sessions ago that you had a job to do, a mission to accomplish. You have done well this far, so let's move on."*

Ian: "Muriel I realize I must start to give you specific details about all this. I repeat that at all times people do have free will; since speaking with you last I have done no positive thinking. I felt sorry for myself, and still regurgitate those old feelings – one can be moody here too. I feel apprehensive about this task and find it difficult to probe. Bill, if you were here you would probably be holding meetings and finding out all the 'goddam' answers in no time! So you need to tolerate my temporary lack of enthusiasm. I know I started this; so will have to finish it. Not to worry – Currie will do so!

"Take care Muriel – we'll talk again. Just send out your vibes and I'll be there – Hell I need a party to 'liven me up'!!"

**Muriel:** As time went on, Ian came to terms with his misgivings, and made up his mind that having arrived in the spirit world, he could bring proof to our world of 'survival after death'. This would bring him a sense of fulfilment, purpose and continuity in the work that he started in the physical life. We had a wonderful line of communication, and the idea of working together to bring forth as much information as possible about how things work in the afterlife was very exciting for both of us. It would also give Ian the opportunity to keep us informed of his progress.

## Reflection

These writings from spirit have been communicated over several years. Due to business commitments, there were long spells when I was unable to give the time to our communications. However it has now been finalised, with Ian's full approval on every aspect of his work.

The professor through his ardent research on the other side explains in an informal way, the knowledge gained since arriving in the world of spirit. I have related our conversations to the best of my ability, with as much accuracy as our method of communication would allow, without exaggeration or distortion. If there was something that I could not understand, or missed because either I was too slow or the frequency was off, I would get back to him later to clarify what he meant. On some occasions Ian would caution that our line was not clear and ask to call back later[2].

**Bill:** The patience and care with which Muriel nurtured Ian through this period of doubt was crucial to the rapport that existed between them. Additionally the patience and perseverance shown by Muriel was apparent as she sought to clarify and expand the descriptions that Ian gave of his life in the spirit world.

---

[2] See, for example, Chapter 5: Energy and Light.

# Research Notes for Chapter 1

## Historical References to Psychic Phenomena

Spirit contact and appearances are not recent occurrences. There exists countless documented evidence of ghostly and spirit appearances over thousands of years, transmitted one way or another. Many are recorded in the Old and New Testaments of the Bible and, according to Fred Archer (1966), the oldest documented evidence was four thousand years ago. Archer, who was also the editor of the *Psychic News* in London, England, cited one of the oldest historical records in the world: twelve tablets found in the ruins of Nineveh, written in cuneiform characters on baked clay, which told of "The Babylonian Story of the Flood and the Epic of Gilgamish", and gives an account of a spirit communicating at a séance.

We also find in the Old Testament of the Christian Bible, the first book of Samuel Ch28 v.7–25, wherein King Saul in disguise, visited a Witch of Endor, where the spirit of Samuel appeared and spoke with him regarding his troubled war with the Philistines. Again we read of the many spirit visitations that Moses had experienced. The most well known of these is that of a voice speaking out of a burning bush as Moses was herding his flock of sheep, stating he should approach Pharaoh and ask that he take the Israelites out of Egypt[3].

---

[3] See the Epilogue and Cerutti (1977) pp 156–60 for many references to psychic phenomena in The Old and New Testaments of The Bible.

# 2
# Crossing the Veil

*"At the time I awoke, I saw a brilliant white light, and felt really pleasant. I found myself in a wonderful clear space, with lots of colour. It was a really peaceful atmosphere."*
– Ian Currie

## The Professor Describes his Passing

**Bill:** For the first of our arranged sessions, I thought it might be easier to tape Ian's conversation rather than Muriel having to write everything. This was a new concept, as she had previously always written down what she heard during a communication, whereas with the taped method she would have to repeat verbally the conversation she was hearing, as Ian's "voice" would not be on the tape. Despite some misgivings, Muriel was willing to give it a try.

The time arrived for our sitting. I felt quite excited as we spoke again of Ian's promise to make contact, hoping he would not let us down. We invited Tricia to sit in and help with taping the session. In preparation we sat in the lounge for a few minutes of relaxation, looking out to the beautiful trees that border the edge of the ravine in our back garden. It was almost eight p.m. and time to commence; Tricia was now ready with the recorder. Muriel started her short meditation and soon made contact with Master Chung her Guide. She acknowledged his presence, and observed that Chung has brought Ian who appeared before her smiling.

**Ian:** "Good evening Muriel, I notice you are attempting to tape our meeting. Hi Bill and Tricia!"

**Bill:** After a warm reunion exchange between the late Professor Currie and myself, I began the session.

**Bill:** *"Ian, I gather from your delightful unexpected communication with Muriel the other day that you wish to give us information about the afterlife. This is really exciting, so why not start from the time of your passing."*

**Ian:** "That is correct I do wish to bring you information from here in spirit, and yes I guess my passing over experience would indeed be a good place to start.

"As I recall I was lying in this hospital room, everything seemed hazy. I was drifting in and out of consciousness. At one point I would say it was as if I was being regressed. The feeling was not what I thought it would be when passing away. First I saw an uncle of mine, whom I knew had died; he was now standing by me. I kind of knew I was dying, and sort of fell asleep again. Then I awoke and saw a lot of people around me and wasn't sure where I was. I saw my uncle again; and also an old professor of mine who had already passed on. He did not converse with me."

**Bill:** *"This professor you saw, what was his name?"*

**Ian:** "Professor Graham! Everything was fuzzy, I think I realized then I had passed on. I started to see colour and thought … *this is it — you're here alright — too bad fellow* — I felt no dramatic change, it was really like falling asleep — no difference — unlike others who have had a very dramatic passing from the earth plane into spirit. For me there was nothing exaggerated, I just drifted in and out of this sleep state.

"At the time I awoke, I saw a brilliant white light, and felt really pleasant and good, and found myself in a wonderful clear space, with lots of colour. It was a real peaceful atmosphere. I just knew I was on the other side of the veil. I felt light in weight, but not like floating, and became aware of the presence of those who were looking after me."

**Bill:** *"You seemed to have seen a lot of colour, what kind of colour did you see?"*

**Ian:** "It was just colour, like watching a movie with different colours coming towards me, really beautiful. Occasionally this white light would surround me, it made me feel good, and everything was so peaceful. I used to believe I would walk through a huge tunnel filled with blazing light[1]. I know that others who have had near-death experiences have related this … *but it did not happen to me!* I guess this tells us there is more than one way to exit the planet. Now I really have left behind all the people I loved in this lifetime."

---

[1] See Chapter 3 and Chapter 6 for a fuller discussion of 'colour' and 'light' in the spirit world.

**Bill:** *"This is all very enlightening Ian. Tell me was there anything akin to a judgement scene that you experienced, like the Christian religions teach us?"*

**Ian:** "No Bill – no judgement scene! Many things concerning the past came forward into my mind, like moving pictures. Then I made a distinct judgement myself, thinking I made so many mistakes, without even trying to put things right. I remember thinking, well there certainly can't be a hell as such; or I might be there! I could not think clearly and had no idea of the time frame of all these happenings. Finally, I realized – *well fellow – this is it … make no mistake,* now you will have to make the best of it you cannot go back and redo stuff. I can also remember saying to myself … damn it … *you should have tried harder!*

"It was my own judgement. There is no place one goes to, where someone sits on a throne or even a chair. There is no committee either. I am sure this will disappoint you Bill, as I know you sit on committees – ha! ha! You are your own judge here … must go now will talk again later. We will have more sessions; this seems to have worked well."

**Bill:** After saying goodbye to Ian, thrilled at what he had just vividly described, we discussed our friend's detailed account of his transition to the spirit world. We felt so privileged to have access to this wonderful channel of information – how exciting for us! I felt that the account of Ian's passing contained important differences from my previous readings. This had felt like a first person conversation (through Muriel) and was describing the case of the spirit of Ian Currie who, as a one-time friend, had kept his promise and returned a month after his demise to give proof of survival.

Before moving on to Ian's fascinating description of how he adjusted to spirit life, it is worth noting that we all discussed the question of taping further sessions with Ian. Muriel expressed concern at having to voice what she was hearing and felt her concentration was compromised with this method of communication; so we decided not to tape further conversations. Muriel was more comfortable with handwriting. Despite this, I must admit that as a researcher into paranormal phenomena, the sudden communication by my late friend and colleague, Ian Currie, had a *'made in heaven'* label on it. What more could I ask for? I now had my own private phone line – hooked up to the spirit world – through Muriel, right here in my home. This was heaven indeed!

## Research Notes for Chapter 2

### Spirit Visitations and the Process of Dying

In the account of his passing Ian made a reference to the spirit visitation of his uncle during the dying process. Also, he knew he had passed on when he saw Professor Graham. I later discovered through one of Ian's colleagues at the University of Toronto, that Graham was indeed Ian's professor in Vancouver.

Other visitations have been recorded in a similar way in other books on death[2]. In a sample survey of some thousands of dying patients, involving 640 medical staff across the United States, Osis and Haraldsson (1977) reported that 83% of those patients had seen apparitions of their families and friends, come to help them during the dying process. One begins to contemplate, just how many millions of people have these similar experiences considering there are deaths every second of the day all over the world.

I also remember an incident from my boyhood days in India concerning my late Uncle Harry, who also had psychic gifts. Once, when I visited him while he was ill in hospital, Uncle Harry told me that a particular bed on the opposite end of the ward would be empty soon, as he had seen spirit visitors around the bed. True enough, the bed was empty the next day; the patient had died. This really mystified and intrigued me in my early years; but I never gave serious thought to it, until my research on Afterlife began in earnest.

Although Ian does not speak about visits to the living from those who have just died, it may be worth mentioning a remarkable incident which was told to me recently when I attended The Toronto Hospital for cataract surgery. A nurse called Conchita, during preparation before the surgery, noticed me reading and making notes from a book about the paranormal. In conversation she related her experience at the Doctors Hospital, Toronto, not long ago, when assisting at a major operation on a male patient. Unfortunately the operation was not successful; and the

---

[2] See, for example, Osis (1977) and Kubler Ross (1974) – both books are highly recommended.

patient died on the operating table. The surgeon asked Conchita to kindly inform the wife of her husband's passing. The nurse phoned and spoke with her at about 3 p.m. Her reply simply was: "I know"... Conchita enquired how she knew – did someone else phone?

"*No,*" she replied quite calmly, *"My husband appeared to me in spirit not long ago and told me not to worry, all is well now – I am at peace with no pain".*

Conchita noted that the time of death recorded was 2.30pm. She gave me permission, to give her name and relate the story. I have read quite a few of these kinds of incidents in my research work.

## Judgement Scene

Ian related a very important point about not experiencing any judgment scene, on his arrival into the spirit world. There are other reported instances whereby on passing over, people also did not experience this. A Monsignor Robert Benson, son of Edward White (a former Archbishop of Canterbury in England), on his passing proceeded to communicate through a psychic friend, Anthony Borgia. In Borgia's (1954) work, *"Life in the World Unseen"*, he describes how the spirit of Monsignor Benson confessed his bewilderment when, in spite of all the religious teachings he gave on earth as a priest, he himself did not experience any judgment scene on his passing.

# 3
## Adjusting to Spirit Life

*"I now have my room/office for study and preparation of lectures. Commitment and dedication are just as necessary in the afterlife as they are in the material life."*
– Ian Currie

**Bill:** The line of communication between Muriel and the Professor was now firmly established. Ian's earthly role as lecturer and researcher into past life regression, would provide the perfect window of opportunity for him to continue his research work from the dimension of spirit. He would be able to share his findings and furnish us with a wealth of first hand information as he journeyed on. But with free will, I wondered if the Professor would be able to accomplish that goal. As time went on and Ian went from strength to strength my fears were well and truly laid to rest and Muriel continued with the questions we had prepared.

**Muriel:** I was sitting downstairs looking out onto the ravine which runs behind our home. I settled into my meditation and almost as though he had been waiting for me Ian appeared in my vision. I noticed that he was wearing a black polo sweater and beige jeans – quite casual.

**Muriel:** *"Hello Ian – nice to see you."*

**Ian:** "Likewise Muriel. It is a beautiful fall day you have – sun shining and all that! I am ready and eager to talk with you."

## Ian Describes his Surroundings

**Muriel:** *"We thought it would be a good time to ask about your surroundings and get your general impression of the terrain Ian."*

**Ian:** "Yes that would be fitting, let's start with surroundings. Just as each soul on the earth is unique and sees things according to circumstances and environment – it is the same here. I have learnt that each soul really does have a very individual impression of life here in spirit. It depends on what plane and level one has reached: how many previous lives one has been through and how much progress was made throughout these lifetimes.

"We have wonderful surroundings and see them as we wish to see them. Colour is phenomenal. Colour is usually encountered at the point of passing through into the afterlife, and we perceive what is within our perception. I think I remarked on this beautiful colour at the time of my own passing. Just as on earth, spirit life is what one makes it; only the physical body is shed leaving the etheric counterpart intact.

"It has been said before by others, so this is by way of confirmation. One can have mountains, valleys, and dales, rivers, houses, greenery and flowers (sounds like a nice piece of real estate don't you think?) – exactly what one's energy level will handle. I will now speak from my own perspective and grade of soul energy.

"I see beautiful gardens here. Regrettably I never had much time for plants, gardens and such. I guess I did not make time for those pleasures and the beautiful things that life on earth had to offer. I know how much you love your garden Bill.[1] I used to admire it when I came over to select books from your library. I imagine when you come over you'll have roses everywhere! It is truly the mind that lives on, so you can picture anything you wish within the realms of your spiritual status. So, as I did no gardening on the planet, Currie has no garden here as yet. Perhaps down the road a bit I will consider that option, but right now my interest still remains focused on my work."

## Setting up Office

"While on the subject of work; you will be interested to know that I have now set up 'office' in my room in order that I feel connected to something, otherwise one drifts around doing nothing in particular. A condition not solely reserved for the spirit world, it also happens in the physical world, don't you agree? As I was saying, I now have my room/office for study and preparation of lectures. Commitment and dedication are just as necessary in the afterlife as they are in the material life.

"So my surroundings are quite pleasant and I can make them how I want by thinking that way, and the good news is – it costs nothing – stingy Currie!! I actually said that, which means I'm making progress! This is one of the benefits of spirit life

---

[1] Ian appears to talk directly to Bill here (also in some of the conversations in the following chapter). This is probably because he was answering questions that had been prepared by Bill.

– we don't have to pay cash for anything – ha! The big challenge is that we earn 'spiritual credits' for what we do towards progress. So be warned and try to rack up some 'credits' before you get here – no help from the banks in this domain! We have to gain credits through our own endeavours and willpower.

"I am able to spend time reading – that is an example of mindset. If I wish to attend a lecture or give one, I can. Also travel – if I wanted to visit Australia I could do that, maybe when the tennis championships are on! You know how I enjoy tennis! Again it is a question of mindset, focus and energy."

## Colour

**Muriel:** *"Ian can you talk a little about colour? I know it is a very important element in the spirit world and you have touched on it briefly."*

**Ian:** "Of course. Yes it is important, as has been verified many times before; colour in the spirit planes is indeed far superior in richness to the colour one sees on the physical plane. I can say that every soul sees colour – how vivid the colour depends on spiritual evolvement. The exceptions to this law are those poor souls who arrive in a self-perpetuated state of darkness, a state known as 'purgatory' or even 'hell' as some may perceive it. This state of mind is brought about by wrong-doings on the earth, a behaviour pattern, which is totally out of line with the purpose of the soul.

"Those who have caused suffering in violation of the natural laws of the universe do not escape this period of retribution.

This is the spiritual law and cannot be changed. Should one escape the laws of man on earth, then one pays accordingly here in the world of spirit for one's sins, so to speak.

"Now – enough of the gloom and doom! Let's get back to the subject of colour. It is in abundance and is the benchmark of our spiritual progress. In the material world, people who study auras see the colour around the outside of the physical body. The aura is indicative of our spiritual well-being. We develop the inner self and gain brighter colours in the auric field as we travel through our life's path. The soul ascends to higher spiritual levels through the process of reincarnation. As progress is made through many lives, the colour of garment cover or cloak in spirit (which denotes the status of spiritual growth) deepens in intensity, and becomes more predominant."

**Muriel:** *"Ian, this has been a long session and I am beginning to tire; besides your vibration is fading and your words are difficult to catch. Let's close now and pick up again later."*

**Ian:** "Right Muriel, I sensed our vibrations were getting faint. We'll talk again soon. Bye."

## Research Notes for Chapter 3

### Colour

Ian speaks about the importance of colour in the afterlife as well as colour in the human aura; so let us expand on this subject a bit further. Tricia, a holistic practitioner who is conversant with colour therapy has provided the following interesting information.

The colours of the rainbow spectrum – red, orange, yellow, green, blue, indigo and violet – are associated in that specific order with the energy centres of the human body through the chakra system. The aura that Ian refers to is the energy field, which surrounds the body and can be seen by some gifted sensitives, such as mediums, mystics, psychics and healers. It is the manifestation of the universal energy field around and within us. Theoretically, the aura is divided into layers, each layer distinguishable through colour. It is possible to recognize impending physical disease by observing imperfections that have manifested in the auric field.

The following excerpt, quoted by Mayer (1956) from Rudolph Steiner's work on Chromatherapy highlights Ian's point about colour and the soul.

*"The substance of the body is air, water, mineral and warmth. The substance of the soul is colour, which is as necessary to the soul as air is to the body. Colour is therefore a matter of great importance and an understanding of it, will throw light upon most of the problems of sickness and healing in the world. The soul lives always in colour, between light and darkness. Man also lives in feeling between thought and will. He is an air being, inhaling and exhaling rhythmically; he is also a light being, unfolding in the light of thought, or thinking which is living in the light."* (p95)

# 4
## Spirit Lifestyle

*"The basic pattern remains the same; the laws of the universe remain the same. Non-believers in the physical world may find it difficult to picture or comprehend the workings on the spirit side. Taking one step at a time makes it easier, and it is good to question and search before acceptance."*
– **Ian Currie**


**Bill:** Ian's description of his 'home base' in the previous chapter was so true to character, just plain simple working space – no twelve-roomed mansion for him. Work and research were the all-consuming elements of his life in our physical world, and it seems that nothing had changed – with the exception of tennis that is, everything stops for the match!

When reading accounts of life in the spirit world, it is important to be aware of just how differently, individual souls create their environment. It certainly appears evident, that the influences of the last earthly existence still remain with the spirit being until that being feels the need to change and move on. Retention of personality is a very significant factor in the transition to spirit life, as we will find out in Ian's descriptions.

After meditating and preparing for the following session Muriel is eventually joined by Ian.

**Ian:** "Good morning Muriel, I can feel your energy stronger. I was just thinking how necessary paper and pen still is even with computers."

**Muriel:** *"Ian I can see you quite clearly; but I'm finding your conversation slightly disjointed – why is this?"*

**Ian:** "Simply because I'm not focusing properly from my end. Maybe it's an imaginary hangover! Can we sit later in the afternoon – your time? Sorry Muriel, will explain later."

**Muriel:** Later that day I decided to sit again and make contact. Ian appears and I tell him to go ahead.

**Ian:** "Sorry for breaking our communication this morning. I seemed to be having a down time. Sometimes I cannot help myself. Here in spirit, I can step back in time and review my past life and earthly failings. Usually I go forward, but then the occasional looking back creeps in. I get those regrets, which bring nostalgia and lackadaisical feelings into my thoughts. However I have pulled myself together and am boosted again. I did commiserate with a friendly soul who went through the same symptoms. He mentioned that I was lucky to be able to communicate with you and keep the energy line open between our two worlds. After giving it some thought, I feel really privileged to be able to communicate. So let's continue with the job in hand."

**Muriel:** *"I am happy to continue, and glad you are feeling better. I am also glad that you shared with us your feelings from the past, and how they can change your energy. Well, I guess that's no different from what* *happens to us here in the physical body. By the way I notice you have changed your spirit attire to a nice red sweater and navy pants. Bill is asking whether you actually did have an imaginary 'hangover'!"*[1]

**Ian:** "I can't believe you can see my clothing Muriel, and you are right I chose the red sweater as part of the 'cheering up process.' I'll have to check out my wardrobe now that I know I'm 'on camera'!!!

"When we get together for seminars or advanced talks on any subject, we also have what could be termed social tête-à-têtes where we can exchange information and views. So Bill, if we want to think 'social evening' at the discussion time that can also include 'refreshments,' whatever your preference might be –'soft' – or even some of the 'hard stuff.' It's all in the mind!

"I can understand that the reader might think this is all fantasy I am relating. However, through mediums and psychics, spirit communicators have given their versions of the happenings and surroundings in the spirit world from their level of awareness. Perhaps I am giving my interpretations using a more modern approach to the afterlife. The basic pattern remains the same; the laws of the universe remain the same. Non-believers in the physical world may find it difficult to picture or comprehend the workings on the spirit side. Taking one step at a time makes it easier, and it is good to question and search before acceptance."

---

[1] See "Research Notes" at the end of this chapter.

## Music

**Ian:** "Strange, but I just heard that bird by your ravine. I think it was a blue jay – it gave a loud screech, which reminded me of just how quiet it is in the spirit world. Of course one can create one's own sound and play 'tapes' in one's head, so to speak. Perhaps I should explain that you could hear any music in the mind, and learn to tune into other souls who perhaps are fellow opera buffs or jazz cravers. For example, if you find another soul who shares your love of a certain type of music, then you can connect and enjoy the same pieces together. Whether you are a professional musician or just love to play a tune (I have been known to strum a few bars myself!), you can get together and have a session of music, dancing or games, shared in close communion with family, friends or just acquaintances. The result – a musical 'soiree', although it could be a musical 'morning,' because who knows what time it is? There is no time here."

## Spirit Time

**Ian:** "Speaking of time, I find it gets a little difficult, as there is no time here like you have. When I want to know the earth time; I watch the clocks when I communicate. I often look at your clock in the kitchen or the family room. Not only are there problems with time, we do not know what year it is, or how many years have passed since leaving the earth. It can be rather disconcerting and hard to come to terms with. Of course it does not bother everyone; I guess we still have our idiosyncrasies.

"One 'guy' (in spirit of course) at one of the lectures I attended, said he was once in the business of cars in France. During his spirit travels in Europe, he used to notice the number plates on cars, and could tell what year the car was registered. In that way he could relate just how long in years he had been in spirit. Quite neat I might say! He also added that to him ten years seemed like yesterday. Time is without hours or minutes, and that's what bugs me the most. Heaven help the real clock-watchers when they arrive. Sorry Bill, you'll have to adjust when you take up residence!"

**Muriel:** *"Ian, with no time structure, how do you plan sleep – or do you sleep at all?"*

**Ian:** "Simple Muriel. If I want to rest or sleep, I relax in my 'hammock' – if I want a bed, I only have to think of one. The big difference is we don't work 9 to 5 over here – ha! ha! One does not sleep at a given time, because it is always light – no darkness, except in the depths of those lower levels[2]. I rest, think, and go over tasks or possibilities for improvement and progress."

## Levels of Friendship

**Ian:** "On this side, like in your world, souls can befriend one another and seek the same level of friendship. We can tune in and seek our level of intellect among spirit beings. Before you know it you have communicated with folk in your own league.

---

[2] See Chapter 14: Levels and Planes for a detailed description of higher and lower levels.

Of course there is almost always someone already here who knows you, which is comforting; so they communicate with you on arrival. On the earth plane, people are brought together through spiritual purpose, like you, Bill and Tricia for example. You three chose to share this particular lifetime with each other, and pursue your goals together and gaining strength from each other.

"I am trying hard in the short time I have been here to collect information for the book; but it takes time to link up the right energy sources. Gradually, I am getting more in tune with my new lifestyle but find myself painfully recalling events in my past life in the physical world that I would rather forget. I try to detach myself as best I can, keeping a steady course by making every effort to keep focused on more spiritual matters. I am sure you understand. Most of my time so far I have devoted to attending lectures from my learned peers who come down from higher planes to do so. Of course I take time out to watch tennis – my favourite sport. My time is my own here Bill, bet that makes you sort of jealous eh? Take it easy and don't work too hard you three. Muriel, thank you for your patience – bye."

## Energy Breaks during Communication

**Bill:** You will have noticed how Ian adjourned the first part of the conversation above. You will also notice a number of breaks in the energy vibration during this and other conversations. Although we could have edited out the interruptions in the energy flow, I thought it was of value to understand how vulnerable the line of communication can be. It is open to the dynamics of the communicator-receiver relationship.

Distractions, physical interruptions and also low energy frequencies: all of these variables can cause weaknesses and breakdowns in the linking up of the energy.

During the course of these conversations with Ian, there were times when a sitting had to be abandoned due to Muriel's ill-health. Her vibrations became too low and dense to be able to make a good clear connection; the energy could not reach the level of quality required for the communication. You will notice that on occasions, Ian mentions the low 'battery' or fading energy.

**Ian:** "Muriel, I am really happy today and feeling light-hearted. I feel much more at home now, I am aware of more colour, which is advancement and so spiritual progress is being made. They say the first three years into anything new are the difficult ones, both here and on the earth. We have to work hard in the beginning to be able to grasp our new circumstances. Now let's see, does Bill have a question for me?"

## Emanuel Swedenborg

**Muriel:** *"It's nice to know that you are feeling good Ian. It makes such a difference to our energy link-up. I notice the lightness in your vibration. Bill wants to ask you about the great psychic Emanuel Swedenborg. Have you heard his name mentioned, or have you by chance met him in your spirit world?"*

**Ian:** "Bill, he has given lectures in one of our universities here. Now I know your minds flip at me using such a term as 'university' but last time I fully explained how our mechanism works, and while on spiritual learning, we can just focus into the field and get on the correct vibration to attend the lecture ......"

**Muriel:** *"Sorry Ian, I lost you there."*

**Ian:** "I was saying ... we seek our own level in our field of work and knowledge. We just have to make some 'phone calls' – send out the vibration – and find out who is lecturing where; if we want some relaxation, we can read – get books from the different libraries. Some of my friends are learning languages. You might ask – 'what the hell for?' Well, when they reincarnate they will possibly recall that particular skill, and make use of it in the next lifetime on earth or whatever. I didn't fully comprehend the workings of our wonderful spirit world, when on the earth plane. I had some idea but not a full picture, which makes it exciting, when I finally got used to being here.

"As always I have left the question behind ... Oh yes Bill, I have attended a Swedberg[3] lecture. I remember him recounting a past life that took place in India. He planted rice in the paddy fields; he really had great suffering and starvation in that lifetime, never got out of the rut and so had a short life. The point of this reference was to highlight the truth, that earthly trauma is part of our path to ultimate spiritual omnipotence. Swedberg also spoke of the changes in his thinking, as each lifetime left its own unique impression on his psyche. I listened to him with great interest – he gave me much to think about.

---

[3] See "Research Notes" at the end of the chapter to explain the use of the name "Swedberg", rather than Swedenborg.

"I reiterate – we can tune into any subject we want. Great teachers like Swedberg are here to teach us; that's what continuous life is all about – learning, understanding, giving and loving others without self gain (other than spiritual credits of course). Monetary values and possessions are all earthly necessities. Here you can acquire all the spiritual growth you need for true spirituality because …… Muriel you are losing me again …… OK. …… I will repeat that …… You can acquire all the spiritual growth you need for true spirituality, because of the non-existence of accumulating wealth, with the exception of acquiring wealth of knowledge and inner peace.

"Interestingly, Emanuel said he intends to stay with us for some time as he is studying further with higher Masters. He is a wonderful orator and goes into this whole inner soul searching in great depth. It is a great thrill to be in his presence, as I was familiar with some of his books during my last earthly stay.

"Muriel you must be getting tired, your energy spark is fading on me, go and have a snack and relax for a while. Bless you."

## Spirit Travel

**Bill:** We now had a fairly clear picture of the surroundings that Ian felt were appropriate to his lifestyle, what he found appealing, and also what irked him in the dimension of spirit, and required time to get used to. He had mentioned earlier about being able to travel, visit and attend lectures of his choice. In this communication Ian expands on this subject and gives us some very interesting information about his activities.

**Muriel:** *"Ian, in previous communications you talked about your spirit travels. You spoke specifically about your love of tennis; your ability to travel to universities around the world, to listen in on what the professors are teaching. Does this mean that any departed spirit can be present anywhere, and see and hear what is happening at any place and time on this planet?"*

**Ian:** "The simple answer is – yes. After you have become acclimatized and accepted the new environment, you then become a free spirit to move around within your spiritual area. The soul is able to communicate with the earth and travel where it has the freedom to do so. There appears to be no end to what one can accomplish spiritually."

**Muriel:** *"Going back to a previous communication, you mentioned that you were going to attend lectures, and listen to intellectuals speak on their respective subjects. Can you tell us about some of the meetings you have attended and who were the spirit folk?"*

**Ian:** "I sat in on a lecture by a great psychic healer. His name was Alfredo and he lived on the outskirts of Rome, in the 1890s. He was born of farm parentage and had a very poor upbringing. He explained that his gift of psychic healing had been carried over from his previous journey on the earth plane a century before. That particular life was in America, and ended abruptly before he was able to use his psychic powers, consequently he retained these powers. In his next incarnation, he returned as Alfredo in order to complete his healing ministry in Rome."

**Muriel:** *"Am I correct in writing that Alfredo had this psychic gift which he had developed in one lifetime; passed on, returned into his next incarnation and carried the gift back with him and brought it to fruition? I presume this means that he was aware that he hadn't used his special talents to the full, so they lay in his subconscious mind ready for use."*

**Ian:** "That's right, clearly we re-incarnate; it is up to each of us to choose whether or not we use our gifts. Life goes with all the challenges that confront us. We tackle them or shy away from them, often making excuses for our lack of commitment. I had opportunities while on the earth which I feel I did not take advantage of, opportunities which in hindsight could have enhanced my progress – well I guess that's life. That is the learning process."

## Trips to Universities

Ian: "Now to the second part of your question. Just how successful was our trip to Universities on your earth planet? We went to Trinity College England, where there was a Professor Baird[4] presiding, who usually lectures at some hall, he was talking on history, also another professor discussing the mind. We also tuned into a South American College where the topic under discussion was 'Space Exploration' – it was about astronauts and how their minds have to be seasoned to deal with their encounters in space. Norway and Sweden were also stoppages at Universities. One of my fellow spirit professors, on the 'tour' was Swedish; so he took us to 'his' University in Sweden where he had been a lecturer in philosophy; his name

[4] See Research Notes.

was Tullenborg. He passed over to this side quite some time ago and was an old man. He has a wonderful conception of man and soul.

"However Bill, I cannot begin to give you all the details we go into on this side of the veil. I have to leave something for you to find out for yourself when you get to our spirit world!!

"Now I am on my way to meet with some European ex-professors (in spirit of course). We plan to chat about the science of the paranormal, and look into the future of how we see the various happenings before us. These professors come from different levels, (I call them 'pigeon holes.') There is one professor who sends out his vibration from another level to us and so we communicate on the same intellectual level of understanding ... all clever stuff!!

"Muriel let's call it a day ... always great talking with you, bye for now."

# Research Notes for Chapter 4

## Alcohol in the Spirit World

It is interesting to note at this stage, the possibility of a hangover, and Ian's explanations. There is a very similar parallel drawn to Ian's findings by the spirit of the late Sir Oliver Lodge. In a book "Nobody Wants to Listen – and Yet!" which was spiritually transcribed by the medium Raymond Smith in 1995 in Malta, Smith quotes Lodge as follows:

*"After my son Raymond [not the author] died in the First World War, he managed to communicate the fact that, in his level of consciousness he could partake of a whisky and soda."* (p144)

Many Spiritualists at that time felt this communication was untrue and that the spirit world did not need the delights of earthly pleasures. Raymond Smith continued: *"In low levels of mind there are more brothels, drinking houses and other similar pursuits than ever existed in earthly conditions. The invisible world has its desire levels in each level of consciousness. What is hell to one may be heaven to another – to each his own."* (Pp144–5.)

Now there's a thought-provoking statement! Incidentally, Sir Oliver Lodge, when living in our world, was a great Spiritualist and psychical researcher – with many books to his credit. He was also a Rhodes Scholar, a scientist and inventor, inventing the 'lodge' spark plug for cars. He passed away in 1940.

## Brief Historical Note on Emanuel Swedenborg/Swedberg

I noticed that Ian in his conversation referred to Emanuel "Swedberg" and not "Swedenborg" as I had called him. When I asked Muriel about the spelling, she answered:

*"That's the name I heard. I didn't query it because at the time I did not realize it was different from the way you had written it."*

I thought nothing more of it until I came to check up some points of reference from one of the many books written on his life and work. The particular book, which I chose was titled *"Emanuel Swedenborg"* by Signe Toksvic (1948). I opened it and read: *"Emanuel was born on January 29th 1688 to Sara Behem, wife of Bishop Jesper* Swedberg *– chaplain to the*

*King's Horse Guards of Sweden."* (p4)

Well, well, there it was; it seems that Ian and Muriel got it right! But how come the book title clearly stated the name as *Swedenborg*? The mystery was finally solved when I came across this further passage: *"History records that when Emanuel was in his early thirties, his father received 'titledom' from the Queen of Sweden, which was a customary gesture bestowed on bishops for their good works. Henceforth the family name was changed to Swedenborg, in honour of the ennoblement, and Emanuel took his seat in the house of nobles."* (p24)

Swedenborg was highly regarded by his peers and subsequent scholars in the academic field. F.W.H. Myers, scientist, professor and Rhodes Scholar from the UK, prominent in the field of psychical research, had this to say: *"To Swedenborg, the unseen world appeared firstly as a realm of law; not a mere region of emotional vagueness and stagnant adoration; but of definite progress, according to the laws of cause and effect; the structural laws of spiritual existence. [...] Swedenborg's God, is the God of a scientist. His God is the essence not only of love, but also of wisdom, which includes order: "God is Order", he said"* [5]

Swedenborg was a man of deep convictions; convictions which were based on years of working meticulously to lay a strong foundation on which to build a working hypothesis, in order to answer the questions – What are we? Why are we? What is to become of us? If there is such a thing as the soul, how is it connected to the body and does it survive bodily death? His books are full of accounts of his extraordinary mystical ability, his scientific research and religious confrontations.[6]

## Professor Baird

A few months later I decided to research Ian's spirit visit to Trinity College, Cambridge University, England. The College informed me, in answer to my query that there was indeed a Professor Baird and his wife, both of whom lectured at the Halls, thus verifying his existence. The mind boggles at this evidence. It leaves me little doubt that the mind, memory and personality lives on[7]. Why then are we afraid to die? This is food for thought and deep contemplation.

---

[5] As quoted in Toksvic (1948), p4.

[6] An excellent introduction to Swedenborg's life and psychic abilities can be found in Toksvic (1948).

[7] Also see Chapter 12: The Mind and its Mysteries.

# 5
# Energy and Light

*"We are energy and light, the light is within the soul.*
*The light shines from the energy, making up the soul.*
*The soul provides the all-important part of civilization's purpose."*
– Ian Currie

## Communicating with Spirit

**Bill:** The level of energy that was needed for the sustained and regular communication in these conversations is best explained in Muriel's own words. In the previous chapter it is clear that communication with spirit demands a lot of energy on both sides. Sometimes Muriel noticed that Ian's energy was decreasing, at other times Ian was aware of her tiredness. This type of communication was a new experience for both of them and Muriel explains how she developed this new ability.

**Muriel:** Before continuing with Ian's next conversation, I feel it is important at this point to explain how I prepare myself for communication.

I am clairvoyant, clairaudient and clairsentient. I am not comfortable with the trance state and prefer to be fully aware when communicating – I 'hear' the words and write them down. When I say 'hear,' I do not mean literally, but rather that 'unspoken' dialogue comes into my mind.

Until the Professor came along I'd never written on a continuous basis, nor kept in constant communication with one spirit being other than my own guide. I have always given readings, and on occasions would write a letter from a loved one in spirit wishing to communicate with their family. However this was a much bigger undertaking and a new experience for me, which was quite exciting. We shared so many communications that Ian became like one of the family, he was so familiar to us. Often he would just come around, make his presence known and comment on something topical or share some other information.

Because of the exacting nature of the communications, it was necessary to assure myself that I was working within the stream of intelligence. I had to raise my energy frequency into a higher level of awareness to ensure as clear a line as possible during the communication. After a short meditation I would expand my energy field until Master Chung came into focus and indicated that my channel to the spirit world was open.

When I am ready to communicate with Ian I sense his presence, then I see him clearly in front of me. I can describe what he is wearing and sense his mood. At this point, I am aware that I have reached the level of thought in my consciousness that will allow me to connect with, and transmit his thoughts.

Once I became familiar with Ian's distinctive energy it was easy for me to pick up his vibration. I could send out a signal to him and vice versa. Over time we were able to perfect our channel, he called it the 'hotline'! It became possible to maintain a clear line for longer periods of time; on the other hand we also learned what would cause weaknesses in the link and became able to detect changes in the level of the energy frequency.

I believe it is possible that cosmic disturbances around our planet can interfere with the quality of the communication, almost like static on a radio frequency can interfere with transmission. Also, if I did not feel too well my energy would be low, or if Ian happened to be in low spirits and below par, then our energies would not resonate, and the line would break up; this occurred on more than one occasion.

There is another point to mention here, and that is, getting out of the way of the communication. Occasionally I would start thinking about what I was writing instead of keeping the line clear for the incoming thoughts that Ian was projecting. Of course the flow was immediately interrupted. Ian always knew when this was happening and I would 'hear' him say "just write, don't think!" and then he would wait for me to get back on track. So these were some of the pitfalls that could hamper clear communication.

Having said all that, I have also experienced times when my energy field would expand dramatically, and I was able to reach the frequency required to gain direct access into the spirit world. At this level I could see into the realms of spirit and be consciously present in the ethereal surroundings. It is almost impossible to describe how this feels. I have witnessed scenes of special celebration in the spirit world that were truly out of this world in every sense. What I cannot determine is whether the ceremony was taking place at that point in time, or whether I was viewing a past or even a future event. That factor is extremely difficult to determine because time as such does not exist in the spirit world.

So I have explained here how I make my connection with Ian. In this next communication we discover how Ian makes his connection to me – which I found quite enlightening.

## Life with a Capital 'L'

**Ian:** "Good morning Muriel, I feel the information we are bringing forth direct from me to you will make very relevant reading for those who are seeking for truth, or looking for confirmation of their beliefs. There should be no doubt in the mind of the reader that life is continuous, in human form and spirit form.

"In your world however, there are many who think spirits float around in oblivion without any connection. We are energy and light, the light is within the soul. The light shines from the energy, making up the soul. The soul provides the all-important part of civilization's purpose.

"We are spirit first: when on the earth plane during our progression, we take on the human element, so we are spirit first, in a human body. I hate the word flesh and use it infrequently. O God, it is all so wonderful. I feel if we could totally conceive the meaning of life – with a capital 'L'– everything would be so much easier; so much is taken for granted, because we do not always see the whole picture – I can relate to that – what more can I say?

"The governing factor of the whole concept is energy i.e. the vibrations and laws that go with our spiritual growth. Another part of our progress is evolution, which entails what we carry forward from previous lives, both on the physical and the spirit level. If we could get the right perspective of eternal life, then our life's path would be approached in a more understanding and orderly fashion.

"To achieve mastery in life on earth, and here, requires preparation, sacrifice, genuineness, and support from others. I remember all the obstacles I hit – on 'doom and gloom' planet – and often felt like quitting. On looking back, I wish I had made better use of the knowledge which was abundantly available to me to deal with life in the human form. However the good news is that spirit is ongoing, and one can continue the process of learning and progressing until the soul decides to re-incarnate again.

"The hereafter presents the opportunity for us to make advancement. One must work through whatever one's particular character has found difficult to handle while in the physical body. A positive attitude can be challenging to cultivate in both worlds. How one copes is inborn and indicative of one's last journey.

"We do not die – we just proceed to the next phase in the ethereal world with the etheric body, i.e. mind, soul, and spirit, intact. Because of eternal life, our energy keeps flowing as it does on earth. Here we still must rest also, though not in the same way as you do. During your period of sleep, while your body is in repose, your mind returns for a short time to the spirit world i.e. its home level – and rests here to regain energy. This energy circuit flows continually in the mind and into the body; it is required to re-energize; thus making sleep so essential for mankind."

**Muriel:** *"Thank you Ian, that's a very good point and well explained."*

**Ian:** "Thank you, and at the risk of repeating myself. I emphasize again, what I said earlier in this communication: the laws regarding spiritual progress do not change. One must follow them in order to climb the metaphorical ladder.

"Upon reincarnation, returning to the physical condition when ready, we must cope with a new life and changed surroundings and circumstances. Remember, the inner being must still adhere to the same rules. This is the challenge of earthly life.

"Oh boy! I think it's time to close on this conversation – if you can call it that – I feel like I've been on a soapbox! Anyway Muriel, your turquoise light is fading so that's it for today."

**Muriel:** *"I could hardly keep up with you Ian, you were really on a roll. I think we'll get an 'A' from Bill!"*

**Ian:** "I like that Muriel. By the way, I feel much more at ease now in my spirit home. Talk to you soon."

## Centre of Energy

**Bill:** After the session with Ian, we had our usual discussion on what I term our 'ethereal mail' from the spirit world. In this last communication, I queried Ian's closing remark – *'Muriel your turquoise light is fading.'* He had never referred to this light before, and I had not come across a similar reference in my research. Muriel was equally puzzled and had no idea what it meant; she had no awareness of this light. It certainly begged the question for another sitting. The next morning through Master Chung, Muriel asked for Ian to meet with her.

**Muriel:** *"Hello Ian, I notice that your energy is different today – there is a lightness to it and you appear to be encased in an aura, like a tent of flimsy opaque light. I also sense the presence of other spirit personalities in your vicinity."*

**Ian:** "You have described the energy surrounding us, which is like a huge cobwebby cloak – I say 'us' because I brought a student group with me. We are in the light because of our collective energy. Your spiritual eye is quite accurate Muriel.

"When I plan to have a 'get together' or class, I send out thoughts so that other fellow spirit beings will pick up the vibration, and be on the same energy line for my message. I pinpoint an area, indicating a circle, then a small radius of energy, starting from me, will link up with whoever plans to attend. When these energies link up they create a powerhouse or centre, which surrounds us with energy and protection; this means that communication is hooked up. So what you called a 'tent' was actually the combined energy vibration, creating a temporary 'room' for our discussion. It's all clever stuff!"

**Muriel:** *"That is fascinating, it's like a sort of spiritual auditorium, with a built in communication system. Tell me Ian, when we speak* *about negative energies here in our physical world, we are usually referring to people who have negative attitudes towards life. Does this same negativity exist in spirit?"*

**Ian:** "Indeed it does. Believe me there are spirit beings here with negative energy, and they may try to push their way into your positive circuit of communication. That is why when we have a meeting or gathering we have to be aware of these damaging energies, make sure we are protected, and so keep the negative forces out of our surroundings.

"Having said that, we need to put this into the correct perspective – there is a difference between a negative force, which is a collective field of contaminated energy, and a poor soul who happens to be having a bad day – so don't let's lump them together. Souls passing into spirit life can bring this negativity with them. It is up to the individual to work at removing this damaging energy from their being. Help is always available and the vibration of love is all around. It all comes back to free will."[1]

## Turquoise Light

**Muriel:** *"Just before we closed our last session Ian, you referred to my 'turquoise light' – Bill is intrigued and so am I; can you explain please?"*

**Ian:** "It is extremely interesting how the circuit of communication works with you. You are like a switchboard, which I plug

---

[1] There is a longer discussion about Free Will in Chapter 13: Spirituality and Religion.

into whenever your line is free. Master Chung is the controller of your connection to spirit – the boss so to speak. I can tell you no one gets past him without permission. Now about this turquoise light; when I want to say, "Hello Muriel," I link in on your frequency, which tells you I'm around. The light is attached to your aura and spirit battery, which is energy – my 'plug' connects to that light, which is a *turquoise light*. Once I have made that contact with you, our frequencies come into line and resonate with each other, and then we're in business!

"Actually today you are a little lethargic; consequently the psychic light is not strong. Soon you will recharge your battery and the energy will flow once again as normal. Will talk soon, bye for now."

## Research Notes for Chapter 5

### Psychic Light

After hearing Ian's explanation of Muriel's psychic light, I did some further research into this perception. Geraldine Cummins[2], a famous trance writer in the early part of the last century, wrote in her (1925) book *"The Road to Immortality"* that the spirit of the late F.W. Myers[3] described, through her, the *psychic's light*. Myers explained this light as a glow from what he called the *vital fluids* around the body of the medium, which he perceived rather as a flame. Myers went on to say that although most humans have this flame, it is weak and invisible to spirit; that only certain individuals, in other words mediums, can make the signal so clear and bright that the spirit communicator can easily sense it. It is the will of the medium, and the state of detached calm, that increases the brightness of the field.[4]

It would be reasonable to assume that Myers was referring to what we now know as the human aura, or in more scientific terms the electro magnetic field, which surrounds the body. Currie defines it as Muriel's turquoise light – both explanations mean exactly the same thing. It is significant to point out that Myers spoke about the light and the energy field long before there was any real scientific evidence to substantiate his words.

### Energy

Throughout the book Ian speaks constantly about energy – spirit/soul energy and physical energy. I think it would be beneficial to explain these energies and what they mean in relation to each other. I have no intention of getting into a scientific discussion on all the various energy fields that exist such as the morphic fields and the fields of gravity and magnetism. These subjects are outside of my expertise.

Energy has been called the source, the universal mind, the God

---

[2] Bill was fortunate to meet her in London, England in 1958.
[3] See Chapter 4 for more detail of the life of F.W. Myers.
[4] See Cummins (1925): p180.

power or if you prefer a more scientific approach – the unified field. All of these titles are applicable depending on one's point of view. Most of us do not see energy, unless you have the gift of discerning the human aura mentioned in an earlier chapter. The energy field can now be measured and tracked by electro dynamic instruments. *"The Electrodynamic Theory of Life"* was published in 1935 by Dr. Harold Saxton Burr and F.S.C. Northrop, both of Yale University School of Medicine. This was the first published paper to recognize and document the existence of the invisible dynamic fields of energy within and surrounding all living matter.

Spirit energy vibrates at a much higher frequency than that of physical energy, and is of a much finer quality. Earthly body energy on the other hand is much heavier and is denser than its spiritual counterpart.

This has been well documented in Valerie Hunt's (1996) groundbreaking work *"Infinite Mind"*. Hunt, a physical therapist and professor of kinesiology at the University of California in Los Angeles, developed a series of experiments to confirm the existence of the human energy field; she was able to gauge the range of frequencies, by measuring the electrical activity around the body. She found that people whose consciousness is focused purely in the physical world registered approximately 250 cycles per second in their energy field. However, Hunt found that people with psychic or healing abilities had much higher frequencies – 400 to 800 cycles per second in their energy field, more than double the count of the previous group. In the case of trance channellers, they operate in a narrow band between 800 and 900 cycles per second. (I believe that mystics actually reach an even higher count.) It is evident by the findings in these experiments that levels of consciousness are defined by the ratio of the frequencies in the energy field.

From the extensive scientific research that has been done in identifying and defining the energy fields, it has been established that the Universe is a boundless field of self-generating energy. From our perspective this is our source, the creation of all living form. We are each attached through our own spirit to this source of higher consciousness and wisdom; and so the spirit energy feeds the soul and creates our individual energy field around and in our bodies. The more developed the level of consciousness becomes – the higher the frequency of vibration. It is important to realize that our spiritual body vibrates at a very high frequency, and that the physical body is condensed and contained within the energy field of the spiritual or etheric body (as we sometimes refer to it). Richard Barrett in his excellent (1995) book says it all in one sentence:

*"It is not the body that has an energy field, but the energy field that has a body."* (p42)

# 6
## Teaching in Spirit

*"Amid the chaos of life, may I alert you the reader to the presence of your higher consciousness? I urge you to take the time to listen to the inner voice, to become aware of your connection to the Universal Power – the Divine Power – whatever you wish to call it."*
– Ian Currie

**Professor Currie Teaches in the Spirit World**

**Ian:** "You may have realized Muriel that I came over into the spirit world before the end of my natural life span. I accelerated my own demise through unresolved issues, which took their toll on my body, physically, mentally and emotionally. I have now come to terms with all of this as time has passed by. Now I continue my life's work here, using all the knowledge gained through intensive study during my last earthly journey, plus of course all that I garnered throughout previous incarnations. I have the good opportunity of sharing my intellect and experiences, working with souls who seek guidance and knowledge. In this way, I am able to remove the sadness that haunted me in the past.

"As Bill knows, I was a Professor of Sociology, research scholar and practitioner in past life regressions. Consequently, I have taken on a similar role here. Let me clarify. I am not an authority on teaching all souls; there are many, many teachers and helpers on all levels and planes. They teach their spiritual knowledge from the same perspective as I do, according to the wisdom accrued through their lifetimes."

**Awareness Therapy**

"I teach souls, especially younger ones who are in need of 'awareness therapy'. For instance a soul may arrive on my level, experiencing an uncomfortable awareness of the inner self, and feeling exposed and vulnerable. This is not uncommon once the sanctity of the rest centre has been vacated, especially if the passing was premature and the personality unprepared for the transition. Remember, the personality does not die with the body; it is retained within the etheric body, flaws and all. It remains as our identity until the point of reincarnation, when the soul takes on a new personality.

"So the bad news is – you are still you – faults included, when you arrive here. The good news is – help is on hand – yes Currie is here – ha ha!! Sorry for the flippancy, but it also proves you can still retain your sense of humour!"

**Muriel:** *"You are in good form today Ian. However you started off to tell us exactly what you teach, and I am still unclear about that. Can you please explain in more detail?"*

**Ian:** "Okay, sorry I digressed. I help souls who are experiencing confusion and having difficulty in understanding their last earthly journey. I help them to see the meaning and the lessons learned in that period of schooling. For example I was talking with a soul called Carol. She explained how, when she passed to spirit, she was really afraid. Her passing was quite horrific – an unfortunate victim of the Hiroshima bombing. Carol remembers receiving help when she first arrived in spirit; but it took her a long time to believe in anything, or try to communicate with relatives already in spirit. Although she knew there was love around her, she was not receptive to it. Of course, as we discussed, *'a long time'* could have been days, weeks or months in earthly time. Because of the trauma and complete disorientation experienced at the time of her death, it took much counselling to bring about a state of realization and awareness that would enable her to move on. Carol was a teacher in Japan, and is now teaching once again here in the spirit world.

"You do understand that once the soul comes into alignment and is attuned to the level of 'being,' it is able to freely decide how to proceed. So my purpose really, is to help a soul to come into balance, in order to make progress. Remember every soul is unique – we are individual beings with totally different energies – there are not two of us the same. When you think about that fact, it is quite incredible. *Millions of souls – yet no two are alike.*

"I also lecture on the origins of humanity, from an anthropological point of view, how the human species has evolved through aeons of time into a sophisticated body. I discuss the development of human consciousness and the role it plays in our spiritual progress.

"When the physical body drops away and we enter the world of spirit, we become aware of the *'loving presence'* everywhere. Unfortunately, while in the earth school, unless one is already highly evolved, the business of living, surviving and dealing with all of life's problems seems somehow to desensitize and block us to the calling of our higher selves. Perhaps, amid the chaos of daily life, I can alert you the reader to the presence of your own higher consciousness. I urge you to take the time to listen to the inner voice, to become aware of your connection to the Universal Power – Divine Power – whatever you wish to call it.

"This does not sound like the 'Currie' that some knew, when in the material world, but I can assure you it certainly is. When I reincarnate into my next lifetime, I fully intend to carry in my soul a more advanced picture of the higher universal intelligence, and the true meaning of life.

"I do not wish to give the impression that you have to come to spirit to learn. You can start right now; your earthly path is your school of learning. You have taken it upon yourself to live in the material world to progress your soul. Never question that you have total freedom of choice to work through your life journey in your own way. We choose the route, and if from time to time, we lose our direction then we must get back on course.

"Well Muriel, did you manage to get all of that down? It's strange when I started this session I had no idea what would finally unravel from my mind. Now I feel really good and glad I got all that said."

**Muriel:** *"I am quite exhausted Ian, your energy was incredible, I can't wait to share this with Bill and Tricia."*

**Ian:** "Thank you, it's amazing to be able to communicate with you so clearly. I realize you have always had the spiritual connection as part of your life. You seem to keep it in the right perspective and I know you must get tremendous guidance all round, you are truly privileged."

## The Professor Meets Young Souls

**Bill:** Ian continued this account of his teaching in the spirit world on another occasion when he brought a group of young souls who had arrived in spirit at an early age. There followed a very interesting dialogue on what these young souls experienced on crossing over into spirit.

**Muriel:** As I sit in the meditation room, I notice Ian standing before me and coming into more direct contact. He has other spirit personalities with him.

**Ian:** "Muriel, we are waiting, the class is here!"

**Muriel:** *"I notice you have company Ian."*

**Ian:** "I have with me these young souls who came to spirit prematurely. I think it would be quite enlightening for you to hear their impressions of how they crossed over. I found that each had in common, a feeling of sensitivity towards the new surroundings and the sensation of still being in the physical body, and attached to the pattern of that life.

"One young fellow, who adored his grandfather, met him, and has remained with him since he came to spirit. A young woman, born in India, died of leukaemia at age 19. As her health deteriorated, she became aware of the fact that she was going to die and interested herself in learning about the afterlife. Her passing was peaceful and consisted of moving through the proverbial tunnel, where she was met by family members and guided to her level.

"Now here are three young souls, sisters Janine, Tracy and Sara. They were killed in a car crash, which happened quickly. Naturally when they arrived in spirit, they tried to find each other. Janine said she died instantly, and floated in space. She then arrived in a large room, where she felt someone soothing her and saying, *'Do not worry it's all right we will look after you.'* Tracy said she did not die immediately, but lay in the car for a short time, and heard a lot of commotion around her. She then drifted into spirit and remembered calling out to her sisters, not realizing what had happened.

"Suddenly Tracy said she saw a light through a misty haze and felt herself propelled towards it; but felt no fear because the light seemed to direct her, which made her feel safe. All the while she kept calling out, *"Where are you?"* to Janine and Sara. Now Sara lived for a few hours in hospital, but already saw the light before her life completely ended. She remembers travelling through a dark area; but the light kept with her. Then she saw colour, felt happy … and fell asleep.

"Here in spirit, helpers work continually to prepare souls to accept their new environment[1]. Teachers give knowledge and assist in spiritual growth. I am determined to continue with this kind of training work, which is my true purpose."

**Muriel:** *"Ian, I have a question for you. At the impact of death, does the soul go immediately to the rest area that you have already explained, before going to the appropriate level, or are there rest and healing areas on each level?"*

**Ian:** "There are thousands of souls passing over from all over the earth world. When bodily functions cease, then the etheric energy automatically takes you to the level according to your status. We cross over into the spirit world in different ways. When a soul arrives here, the procedure will vary, depending on the physical condition.

"If for instance there was a long painful traumatic death, this soul would go into a rest area on his or her level, until all the trauma and pain is shed from the psyche. The soul then proceeds into its spiritual environment on that same plane and level. I want to talk more about planes and levels in the spirit world, but we will leave that discussion for another time.[2]

"Muriel, I would say that your channel is open and clear today. You are well protected by spirit, which is wonderful. I told these young spirits here that we have a private hotline! Will leave now, regards to Bill and Tricia."

---

[1] Also see the section on 'Children in Spirit' in Chapter 8: Reincarnation.
[2] See Chapter 14: Levels and Planes.

## You are Your Soul

**Bill:** In the next extract the Professor states unequivocally, and without hesitation that "You are your soul"; with no if, but, or maybe. It is just so exciting to receive such profound clear-cut information from this wonderful source. We feel truly blessed, because Ian is validating everything that we have come to know and fully accept, through our own personal experiences and research projects. It is our wish, that through this book, you also might feel the thrill of validation of your own thoughts and beliefs. The following short text from Professor Currie is so pointed and succinct on this subject that we felt it should be set apart, rather than be included within a regular conversation.

> **Ian:** "Natural law here in spirit governs our spiritual progress, which is contained within the soul – that statement is fact not fiction. The universe is in total control of our capacity to breathe, think, know and 'be' – you are your soul – your spirit is the connection between you, and the source of your 'being.' You have to believe and trust in this information, which has been written about and recounted, by the great teachers of our world through generations. We are connected with the Universe – and have been from the beginning of time. Our life's challenge in the earthly world is to keep in contact with our source, as we journey along the path in a truly spiritual way.
>
> "I have talked with some souls here who admitted frankly, that they had a problem seeking or acknowledging their spiritual right, because they felt that to do so would restrict them to a life of pious righteousness. As a result of this erroneous thinking, they did not avail themselves of spiritual guidance

and adopted a – 'don't want to know – I'll take my chances' attitude in their lives.

"Now, the point we are trying to make in this book, is to let people understand – there is continuous life – for which we are eternally grateful. We have the opportunity to keep progressing, increasing our knowledge, and hopefully our wisdom along the way. Just being part of this wonderful universe, – believe me, when you get here and really understand what life is about – is such a wondrous experience."

# 7
# Masters and Guides

*"Guides are governed by their duty to individuals on the earth plane. Masters are teachers of the soul."*
— Ian Currie

## Inauguration of a Philosopher

**Muriel:** I am sitting in the meditation room when Ian suddenly presents himself.

**Ian:** "Good morning Muriel, sorry I zoomed right in. I'm getting really good at it. I have just shown you what I wore to a big inauguration of a philosopher who was inducted into a higher plane. It was quite a ceremony and all those attending wore their spiritual robes of colour. The colour here is pure, and much brighter than your material colours. It was a wonderful scene resembling the pomp and splendour of an earthly ceremony, though more intense. In the spirit world, a farewell occasion is commonplace upon reaching a certain level in soul status, and the moving to a higher realm. Masters from the realms of higher intelligence attend these occasions, coming mainly from the same level as the graduating soul is entering into."

**Muriel:** *"Ian, I seemed to have lost concentration. I got so excited imagining this scene as you were describing it. Sorry if I've put you off your track."*

**Ian:** "The soul making the grade was an Egyptian philosopher. He was a seer and archaeologist from the 16th century."

**Muriel:** *"Sorry I am having trouble with our wavelength; I now seem to be seeing this spirit entity. As a result, I'm aware of weakening our line; but I must describe him to you, as it is important for me to confirm. He is very tall, dark and wearing a neat rolled headband with a white heavy cloak behind him. I am picking up from the vibration, that while he was on the earth plane his garments always had black and gold on them. He was a marvellous man and could see far into the future. Although he dwelt in Egypt, he lived in a mountain area and had a school of learning there. I am getting a name from him – Joseph Mulki[1] – sounds something like that."*

**Ian:** "Muriel that was really something to pick all that up."

**Muriel:** *"I must get back on to your energy. Apologies for the distraction Ian, but I just could not resist following through on that vision. His appearance was really striking and I could clearly see the picture in front of me."*

**Ian:** "Do not worry Muriel, I am still here. Any movie producer would give his right arm to be able to film these ceremonies. The colour from all the attendees is radiant and quite breath-

---

[1] It is possible that future research may verify the existence of Joseph Mulki as a sixteenth century archaeologist.

taking. The higher Masters' cloaks are always beautiful; the colour portrays rank, and is a form of decoration or reward for spiritual achievement. It shows service to humanity on the earth plane, coupled with dedicated service on the spirit planes.

"I guess we should get back to the job in hand. I am sure you have a subject for discussion, so we had better get on to it before 'you know who' tells us off!"

**Muriel:** *"Yes, you are right on both counts, and coincidentally what you've been talking about and Bill's question are on the same theme – Masters and Guides – who are they and what exactly do they do? Let's continue on from there."*

## Guides

**Ian:** "Good, let's talk about Guides. Everyone on earth and in spirit has guides, who work from spirit, ordained by the Divine power. Their purpose is to help us through life's journey, to be the liaison between your inner-self and the spirit world – but not to interfere with free will. These guides also make progress on their own behalf, by working to help mankind progress further with life's pattern.

"It is also interesting to note that the guide forms a partnership with whomever they wish to accompany through their earthly incarnation. On earth these guides are sometimes referred to as 'angels'[2].

---

[2] Ian does not expand on the debate as to whether guides and angels are the same, or different.

"Muriel, when we decide to reincarnate, we meet with our guide before being reborn, but once we become embodied again, we do not remember this event. Our task in the physical world is to develop spiritual awareness to enable us to tune into our guides and enlist help with life's many problems and challenges. In a way it's like having a mentor with whom we can communicate on both a material and spiritual level.

"Mind you, guides could land amiss if the person they chose goes through life totally unaware of their presence; this means the guide has wasted his or her time. I guess when that protégé returns to spirit, the guide would be standing by to say – 'what a 'B' waste of time you were – ha!' – However, the guide does receive credit for trying to get through to an individual, who was for whatever reason unable to develop in that capacity during that particular incarnation."

**Muriel:** *"Sorry Ian, I'm losing your vibration again, there is a bit of distraction here. I heard a fire engine race by with the siren blaring, which disturbed my concentration. Just give me a moment or two ...... Okay, go ahead I'm with you."*

**Ian:** "Muriel I know, I also heard that siren. Well now, on a more serious note, I was saying that every soul who walks the earth has a guide, in fact quite often more than one. Whether you are aware of the true nature of this guiding presence, is less important than the knowledge that you have access to a source which is outside of your five senses i.e. your sixth sense, it is in this dimension that your sense of knowing is developed, and answers to questions are forthcoming, this is where the guidance manifests. So do not think because you are unaware of the identity of your guide, that this denies you access to your source.

"At the level of the soul you know your guide – mentor, counsellor, angel – whatever label you use. How you connect is a highly individual personal act, and is not confined to a specific method. I hesitate to pinpoint any particular regimen but suggest that you go for what works for you, and what seems comfortable. Remember this is all part of the learning process and the spiritual journey.

"Consider great leaders such as Gandhi, and Martin Luther King, who travelled through their lives spreading the spiritual message, and performing heroic acts of humanity. We realize that these souls and others like them arrived on the earth plane with a blueprint already rich in wisdom, love and spiritual knowledge, and of course with compatible guides of an equally high level to assist and support them in their chosen service to mankind. This also applies to ordinary men and women who lead exemplary lives and perform heroic tasks on a daily basis without ever making the spotlight. These great personalities continue their work in spirit on another level of 'being.' Believe me, it is one long spiritual journey, evolving in both worlds."

**Muriel:** *"Ian, it is said that some spirit personalities choose not to identify themselves when they communicate to the physical world. Why is this?"*

**Ian:** "Yes this is so, spirit communicators sometimes conceal their true identity when they communicate, and prefer to use a pseudonym so to speak. Most of the more eccentric ones were famous personalities during their last lifespan on the earth, and on passing over have continued to do a great job of communication from spirit, providing valuable spiritual information and giving healing service. Sadly, there is a certain scepticism associated with the idea of a famous personality who is discarnate communicating with the earth plane through a medium. This could be construed sometimes as sensationalism or exploitation on the part of the medium who is channelling this personality. So in the interest of all concerned it is beneficial for the spirit personality to remain somewhat anonymous."

## Healing Guides

**Ian:** "Healers in the physical world more often than not, work in conjunction with healing guides through the same structure of communication. The guides make contact from spirit and work in cooperation with and through the healer, who is often given information about the condition of the person requiring the healing energy. The power of spirit has healed the ailments of humanity throughout our history. Guides also specialize in their particular field of healing work – be it physical, emotional or spiritual. While on earth, I knew several mediums who had their own group or band of healing guides. Each guide had expertise in dealing with specific problem areas – such as bones, nervous conditions and others who gave strength to patients in cancer therapy. So you see there are very powerful forces in and around you that can be used to balance and heal the body."

## Ian's Guides

**Muriel:** *"Bill wanted to ask you if you were aware of your guides in your earthly life, and did you meet with them again when you passed over?"*

**Ian:** "Yes Bill, I did know about my guides. I had two, an Egyptian, and a monk from the 13th century. I met both on arrival this side of the veil. The Egyptian was the strongest; he was my mentor, 'Solomni' dating back to 1000 B.C. – he is still available to me and we talk on occasions. His mission at the present time is to study and extend his own spiritual autonomy. When I reincarnate it will be his choice if he wishes to allocate himself to me.

"You know it is possible that I might have the option to become a guide myself, instead of reincarnating. I certainly feel I have the qualification; but somehow I do not think it is my forte this time around. However when the time comes for me to make a decision, I am sure I will know beyond doubt where my path lies. On this note I will close, and talk about Masters next time. Take care Muriel … Bye for now."

## Masters

**Muriel:** The next day I awaited Ian's arrival to speak on Masters as he suggested.

**Ian:** "Muriel I am here, and ready to continue where we left off. We will speak about Masters in the spirit world.

"Knowledge is dispersed through growth in learning. It is analogous to attending a University – the further you go, the more knowledgeable the teacher in that academic field, because of the depth and scope of the research and study. The same principle holds true here. If you want a definitive answer you require it from a master of that particular subject. Masters are great philosophic teachers, who come from higher planes. It takes many lifetimes to reach that plateau of perfection. In comparing Masters, there are different degrees of spiritual progression. All of them have reached their respective planes – and levels within. This is in accordance with the knowledge and spiritual acumen acquired through centuries of time.

"Firstly, many have reincarnated and evolved from the beginning of man's existence, developing their spiritual 'bodies' through each lifetime. Masters are teachers of the soul. They communicate their philosophy to the world through the mediumship of highly sensitive individuals on the earth plane."

**Muriel:** *"I know that there are certain Masters whose mission it is to make their wisdom available to us here in the material world. Bill wanted to verify that you also can obtain information from Masters who come down to your plane and level from time to time, and give lectures. Do you know how many planes there are?"*

**Ian:** "In the spirit world Masters are the hierarchy, the spiritual educators. It is their task to dispense knowledge down through the planes by means of seminars. There is a structure to the system governed by the universal laws. So yes Bill, the Masters impart their spiritual findings to us. The higher the plane the Master is on, the higher will be the level of wisdom that comes forth – far beyond our current understanding.

"I am learning and furthering my knowledge by sitting in on lectures given by some of these learned scholars, and hopefully will be able to share it with you and our readers. I am closing now Muriel – will verify the question of planes next time – bye."[3]

---

[3] See Chapter 14: Levels and Planes.

# 8

# Reincarnation

*"When the time is right, the soul passes back through the veil in order to make further progress in the earth school. The process consists of nurturing one's own development, and carrying out the destiny, karma or blueprint one chooses to follow."*
– Ian Currie

**Bill:** This conversation took place over the course of many days and provides a fairly comprehensive view of many aspects of reincarnation and the process of rebirth. It appears that Ian had to do a substantial amount of research to bring us this information. It reminds us that, just because we have passed into spirit, will not in itself mean we suddenly know everything there is to know, and as Ian has pointed out the learning process is long and ongoing.

**Ian:** "Hi Muriel, I am in a saner frame of mind today. I am sitting at my desk in the office so that I am better focused to answer your questions more directly – so fire away!"

**Muriel:** *"I'm glad you are more focused today because this question is a big one … First, when do souls decide to reincarnate, and do they choose their parents? Second, at what point in pregnancy does the soul enter the womb?"*

**Ian:** "All right, yes this is a big subject so let's get started.

Reincarnation is a complex event. As I understand, the soul remains in the spirit world for as long as it needs. Some souls require many years (gauged time) before attempting another go into the earthly life path, because they are safe and happy here. However, reincarnation is the learning process of spiritual progression, and eventually they must leave the comfort zone and return to the physical body. When the time is right, that soul passes back through the veil in order to make further progress in the earth school. The process consists of nurturing one's own development and carrying out the destiny, karma or blueprint one chooses to follow.

"Another aspect of my teaching is to educate and counsel spirit people who are close to entering the reincarnation process, so that they have more stability when they return to another life. I can hear the 'sceptics' on the subject saying, "We don't remember anything of that nature when we are reborn into the physical dimension". This is true to a point, but it's all there deep within the mind. During the next life, if we wish we can pull out that information through different methods such as meditation and regression. All knowledge gained through time on earth we bring back to spirit, while here we gain more knowledge if one so desires and automatically take it back to earth. Everything is stored in the mind from each lifetime. As we age, before passing to spirit we can lose memory through various health issues and illnesses; but this is only a temporary impairment. All information is stored intact for use when needed at a future time.

"Once the decision is made to reincarnate, the spiritual laws come into effect and the process starts to evolve. The soul begins consultation with guides who will mentor the incarnating soul through the new journey. I mentioned the role of guides when we had the session on Masters and Guides."

## Choosing Parents

**Ian:** "The soul chooses the parents that will provide the background and/or culture for its purpose. While in spirit waiting to reincarnate, the personality is still from the previous life and will remain so until the soul is ready for rebirth into the physical plane. Personality then becomes a memory, a past life experience. Once in the womb, the characteristics of the new parents begin to take effect. Now we start all over again to build resources for another walk on the earthly path."

**Muriel:** *"Does the DNA of the new parents interfere with the gifts, talents and spiritual knowledge held within the subconscious of the newborn?"*

**Ian:** "The parents are there to supply a home – a physical body for the soul spirit; by 'home', I don't mean all the material stuff! Heck, the expense they have to bring up and educate kids – there I go again, I haven't lost my last life's thoughts about the cost of living! Huh! ...The purpose of Eternal Life is advancement. It would not make sense if the newborn soul lost its spiritual knowledge and special gifts through the DNA of the parents.

"Perhaps I should make a distinction here between the level at which the soul reincarnates from, and the level of human life, to which that soul commits to before being reborn. A soul already developed in understanding and in harmony with the Divine Power, may choose the most humble parents and incarnate into a lowly earthly life, full of poverty and suffering; or decide on a physically challenged existence.

"These are only two examples of many different scenarios the soul might undertake in order to gain further 'spiritual credits' (as Bill so aptly terms them). So, level does not refer to a human standard of life. The level of integrity within the soul, in dealing with earthly circumstances, is the key to all of this; whether royal or peasant, the truth is that rank and position mean nothing. *It is service to mankind, love, and compassion and in some instances deep humility that brings reward to the soul.*

"Now Muriel, let's see where we are at, I think I got side tracked! Yes, parents and DNA – let's continue. At the beginning of the new journey, you take on another personality and possibly a different gender. The DNA of the parents will probably add other attributes. You may not get the chance to use the latter; but they are stored in your subconscious power box, ready for use in future lifetimes. This shows up in children who display talents far beyond their tender years, resulting in a child prodigy or genius. It all adds to a level of high spiritual achievement. Remember, you are firstly a spirit being who takes on the material earthly 'cloak' poetically speaking, in order to keep the soul progressing and reaching various goals for inner satisfaction.

"Finally Muriel, the divine light surrounds us here in the spirit plane. You can figure it out any way you like; but please, do not close your mind to the truth – we are all linked to the

Divine Power. Take heed to what I have said, especially the point of spirituality, which is achieved by following the spiritual laws and helping others with good intent. It will lead you to your rightful path.

"I will close now, it has been a long session and you must be getting tired Muriel, your energy is fading. We will talk about conception next time."

## Conception and the Soul

**Ian:** "Okay Muriel, let's continue with our discussion about re-entry into the physical body. Your question was as I remember; at what point does the soul enter the womb? The answer is – *the spirit/soul unites with the seed at the time of conception – right at the point of fusion.*

"Now let me qualify this statement. The spirit is the soul energy and so is linked at the moment of bonding. The spirit feeds the soul during pregnancy, and the mother feeds the body for the growth of the baby. If, as some people believe, the soul bonding did not occur until the time of birth, that would mean the foetus would be growing without the soul connecting with the physical body.

"As we have spoken about many times in previous conversations, we are primarily immortal. The human body is merely a vehicle for the expression of the soul therefore that soul must resonate with that forming body within the mother, and for that matter with the mother also. During pregnancy, the soul goes through a period of transition, gradually losing awareness of its spirit home; but I hasten to add, *not its connection,* which is a very important point. The integration of the soul with the foetus is a gradual process; however I reiterate that the soul/spirit is united instantaneously with the embryo at the moment of procreation. It is protected from unwelcome intrusion by any other entity, until the embryonic process is completed. As the embryo develops, the physical body becomes denser and the energy frequency of the soul must harmonize with the density of the foetus.

"The energy frequencies of spirit are much higher and lighter than those of the earth, and so much preparation is required by the incoming soul, in order to become compatible with the lower vibration requirements of the human body. At the time of birth, there is a final acceleration of consciousness, as the newborn is introduced to the world and becomes aware of its new surroundings. The soul has gone through the natural route of acceptance, and now belongs with the parents of its choice.

"If I may philosophize for a moment – the human body is a wonderful machine, exquisitely designed; the brain is an intricate power box. However, soul/spirit is what turns the human *body* into the human *'being.'* I think I put that rather well – don't you? Very concise – this is a change from me rambling on, as I am prone to do.

"Muriel, I am making a hasty exit now before Bill comes up with queries about fertility drugs, surrogate mothers and all the rest. It took me long enough to procure and prepare the information on the process of birth. I'm way out of my league with the other stuff ... Thanks."

**Bill:** I did have a good laugh when Muriel told me about Ian's abrupt departure after his conversation. I don't blame him! I have the feeling the spiritual Hierarchy are still trying to work out the rules on these happenings!! It is interesting though to realize that in spirit, one does not automatically know everything. Research has to be done to gain information on subjects outside of one's current knowledge, once again showing how our two worlds are akin to each other.

## Children in Spirit

**Bill:** We decided that this would be a good time to ask Ian about children in the spirit world. It is always a matter of great concern to parents who have suffered this loss, to know that their beloved child is safe and being cared for in spirit.

> **Muriel:** *"When a baby or young child dies, what happens to that soul when it returns to spirit, and can it communicate with the parents?"*

**Ian:** "The baby arrives here for whatever reason it has ceased to exist on the earth. It has not been aware of what has really been happening because this soul was still partly living in spirit. The brain/mind had not been set into understanding its new life, and further, has not had the chance to make any spiritual progress. Now the soul discovers itself back in the world of spirit, without coming to the awareness of the earth school. The baby returns to its appropriate level at the time of the incarnation. It then has to grow in spirit, and it will automatically take on its new DNA, because of the new parents at the time of birth. The personality then develops in spirit until it reincarnates again.

"Now you ask the question, how can it communicate with earthly relations if this soul is only a baby? This soul has rightfully returned to the area of spiritual growth from whence it came. The baby will only appear when required by the earthly family, as a sense of baby energy and in some cases, in vision as an infant. But remember the soul has returned to its rightful place and level in spirit, and will resume its spiritual journey. When an older child comes to spirit, whose personality has formed (by the age of seven I believe), it will continue to grow and thrive in an atmosphere of love and protection. I trust I have explained this clearly Muriel?"

**Muriel:** *"Yes I think I've got that down okay. If I find I'm confused, I'll get back to you for clarification."*

**Ian:** "Good enough, I admit it was a little difficult to follow my train of thought on that one. However we will press on if you are agreeable, as I have more information to share on this subject.

"Now I believe it is possible, that a soul, which has succumbed to the stillborn baby or miscarriage, may again reincarnate into that same womb when the time is right. It would be reasonable to assume in this case, that the need for this soul to be united with these particular parents is the most compelling factor in the reincarnation; and would be a very necessary component in that new life.

"This is rather a difficult part of reincarnation to understand, and I do not profess to know all the answers, nor am I conversant with all of the different scenarios that could take place at that time. Babies and little ones who pass over to spirit are cared for and nurtured until they are sufficiently developed to move on and continue their rightful paths. It is the same loving process as takes place in the physical world."

**Muriel:** *"Thank you Ian. It is most comforting to have this confirmation, and to know that the spirit world is indeed the beautiful loving place we imagine it to be."*

## Pets in the Spirit World

**Bill:** Many people can tell stories of devoted pets and their heroic activities with their owners. Sometimes people believe that the spirit of their pets has passed into a new pet. We decided to ask Ian about this.

**Muriel:** *"Ian, I'm sure the readers would like to know what happens to their pets when they die. Do they exist on the same levels and planes in the spirit world as we do? Do they meet up eventually with their owners?"*

**Ian:** "There is a very short answer to your question Muriel, no to the first part and yes to the second part. However, I wouldn't dream of depriving you of my knowledge on this subject. So here is the long-winded version!!

"Animals are not on our spiritual levels. They have a life energy that connects them to their own collective spirit world. Each species carries a blueprint of evolution, within what we call the animal kingdom. Now, do the owners when they pass to spirit see their pets again? Yes indeed they do. The love radiating from the owner brings the animal right into the field of that vibration."

**Muriel:** *"That's interesting Ian. Often during a reading, I see a dog or cat in spirit, running around or sitting at the feet of my client. Usually I can give a good description of the animal; much to the delight of the 'owner'."*

**Ian:** "Yes, that is a perfectly feasible happening Muriel. Again it shows the pull of that love energy. It's amazing how strong that bond becomes, between family members and their pets, and losing that animal is akin to losing a close family friend.

"The important difference in this scenario is the fact that pets receive love and care, through interaction with human beings. They return the love in the form of devotion and service. This bonding develops in the pet a level of connectedness with the human psyche, which distinguishes it from its wild, instinct-driven counterpart.

"These animals do not advance and reincarnate into a higher level. They do not progress individually, but evolve as a species or group. The only distinction I can make is that the intelligence develops from one incarnation to the other. Often you hear someone say: I am sure my dog (or cat, horse, whichever) knows exactly what I am saying; and yes, I'm sure this is so. Animal pets live in close proximity to human beings and interact with them. This stimulation produces a higher level of intelligence.

"The stories about pets performing heroic acts of endurance, devotion, and bravery, in order to protect or save their masters could fill volumes. One just needs to think of guide dogs for the blind, and animals in the police and fire services to illustrate the point. In the spirit world no acts of sacrifice go unrewarded.

"I trust that this explanation will enlighten our pet lovers and put their minds at rest that pets are taken care of, and will certainly be around for a reunion."

**Muriel:** *"Thank you Ian, I'm glad you decided to give us the benefit of your 'unedited' version. It was most enlightening. I look forward to our next get–together."*

## Research Notes for Chapter 8

### Near-Death Experiences with Pets

At a 'Beyond the Brain' Conference held in Cambridge University, England in 1997, Dr. Kenneth Ring, a well-known paranormal researcher related a remarkable story about a blind man having a near-death experience with his seeing-eye dog. He explained how the owner with his seeing-eye dog was knocked down by a hit-and-run car. The dog lay by his side watching over his master. At this point the blind man entered into a near-death experience (NDE). He was aware of himself drifting away towards a bright light, and noticed that his faithful dog was running behind him, agitated and in a state of confusion, as though trying to follow his master's spirit body. The spirit of the man of course eventually returned to his body where the dog was lying patiently. Dr. Ring had researched this case, and taped the story from the blind man after he recovered from the accident.

In conclusion, this incident tells us that the dog had a psychic sense to follow the spirit body of his master, and yet returned and stayed by his body until help came. Further, that someone blind from birth, suddenly had vision during his near-death experience – which was the point of Dr. Ring's presentation in his research work.

# 9

# Spirit Communication

*"Information from spirit is completely controlled by levels of energy vibration. The quality and clarity of the energy channel is fundamental to the accuracy of the transmission between the transmitter and the receptor."*
– Ian Currie

## Psychics and Spirit Contact

**Bill:** I was thinking the other day about the different methods of communicating with the spirit world. There are trance mediums that allow a spirit entity to take over the voice box and speak directly through them. There are those who do automatic writing where the hand of the medium is taken over by the communicating spirit, who then writes his or her own message. Materialization mediums may exude ectoplasm in order for a spirit being to manifest a physical image, and of course we have the psychics and mediums like Muriel, who communicate through hearing, seeing, and sensing those in spirit. It is obvious that these people have a natural heightened sense of awareness and ability to tune in to the world beyond. Ian had indicated that he wanted to discuss the subject of communication from spirit, and to explain further about this process.

> **Ian:** "Information from spirit is completely controlled by levels of energy vibration. The quality and clarity of the energy

channel is fundamental to the accuracy of the transmission between the transmitter and the receptor.

"To continue with this subject, we might ask, why can't everyone communicate with his or her nearest and dearest – on either side of the veil? Well, it is a fact that all human beings possess the capability to receive information from spirit, but somehow people in general are not at all comfortable with this idea. I can tell you that first hand – I know how much opposition I met in the process of my research work in the material world. Any subject that had even a suggestion of the occult was often viewed with disparagement. As you have pointed out Bill, there are special beings like Muriel who have heightened sensitivity and a refined energy resource, which they can naturally tap into. Energy vibration and spiritual levels are important elements in communication between our two worlds.

"The whole concept has to fit into place. Metaphorically speaking, batteries must match and plugs must fit into the right sockets to provide the energy link. I know it seems ironic that sometimes two people, such as husband and wife who were close all through their physical lifetime and had a wonderful relationship, have difficulty communicating with each other when one or the other passes over. One has to consider the belief factor, and also recognize that some people do not understand the intrinsic nature of the communication. Muriel, you and I are fortunate to have for the most part, a clear and unobstructed line for our talks. However as we have sometimes experienced, fragmented thinking, lack of focus and low energy can all affect the quality of the channel from time to time."

**Muriel:** *"If I may interrupt you here for a moment Ian. I want to say that the question of trusting the information received from spirit is crucial to the one who is directly receiving the information. When I was developing as a medium I was fortunate to be invited to attend a teaching circle for development at the Spiritualist Association of Great Britain. The first lesson I learned was to trust my channel, trust my guide and never to doubt the validity of the information I was being given – a valuable lesson, which I have practised ever since."*

**Ian:** "Yes indeed Muriel, trust is very necessary. Spirit communication is not an exact science, but nevertheless it is within the reach of those who desire to make contact. From the earthly perspective, it requires practice and must be supported by an unwavering belief that your loved one is still with you, albeit in a different form and that the transfer of thought between you is both possible and desirable. These factors are pretty much a prerequisite to setting up a line of communication with someone in spirit.

"Scientists in both worlds have been trying to bring the two dimensions closer together. For some years now they have been experimenting on the computer, believing that spirit images can be reflected on the screen[1]. One never knows, perhaps I will eventually be able to show myself on that computer screen once the technique has been developed – which may not be too far away. In that case I will need some warn-

---

[1] A few years later Muriel and Bill were invited to be part of a major research conference in the US on energies and vibrations (Higher Reality) to develop the projection of spirit images onto a computer screen through Instrumental Transcommunication (ITC). Muriel began discussions to explore work in this field but she was unable to pursue this further because of her illness.

ing in order to look my best ha! Wouldn't that be a quantum leap in communication?"

## Information from my Level

"I should make it clear that the information from my level on the spirit plane is correct, as I see it, through my research work and experiences. In addition I have obtained knowledge through attending lectures presented by higher Masters, and experienced evolved spirit professors in their fields of expertise.

"But Muriel, having said all that, without doubt there is some diversity in the information received from the spirit world to the earth plane. Even great writers of the past, who did research work in the material world, received slightly different answers to the same questions. This happens because of the diverse spiritual and human lifetime experiences of the spirit communicators. In other words, the overall explanations stay the same, but the details may vary.

"Here is an example: in the physical world you may have two witnesses to an accident. They see exactly the same scene, but their statements are at variance with each other, this occurs simply because of the individual's interpretation and perspective of 'reality.' The point I am making is that the information from my spirit plane and level is correct, as I see it. It is as I perceive it – profoundly and perfectly clear-cut, from me to you, with no additions or deletions. I do not wish to blind you the readers with science; but give you the simple truth.

"The main purpose of this work is to bring confirmation and proof that life continues after physical death; that life is ongoing and extremely productive in both worlds although they are so paradoxically different – one in dense material form and the other nebulous. If this book even starts you thinking, then I have done my part towards your spiritual growth. Remember we have free will to choose all through life's journey. It is a long road to the perfection of the soul and the final achievement of the ultimate spiritual reward. It is a gift to be able to keep in touch with spirit during the earthly interludes of our existence, but it is also important to maintain a stable balance between the human element and the spiritual.

"I have a lot of research to do here in spirit, my inquisitive mind will keep delving, and there is so much to learn in both worlds. We must keep the spirit active and alert, and above all have love for our fellow beings. It's been good talking to you Muriel, as always. I look forward to our next tête-à-tête – you do have a dreary November day."

## Spirit Impostors and Poltergeists

**Bill:** Ian's talk on levels of communication and the logistics of channelling started us thinking about different types of communication, such as spirit impostors that claim to be someone they actually are not. Also Poltergeists: they create violent energy around certain unsuspecting human beings. We decided this would be a good subject for discussion at the next sitting.

**Muriel:** I am waiting for my psychic energy to pick up a clear picture of Ian. I soon see him; he is wearing a soft green sweater and pants. I compliment him on such a nice vibration.

**Ian:** "Yes Muriel, I love changing colours because we can project or reflect anything we desire within reason; of course there is no budget to consider as you have in the physical! By the way did you know that continuous change takes place here in the spirit world because of the different energies that come to spirit? We who are domiciled in the afterlife do communicate new ideas to the earth plane – to science and other areas of earthly establishments, for progress. We keep working to make the world a better and happier place for future generations."

**Muriel:** *"Thank you for that information Ian. May I just pose a question on a topic which Bill and I have been discussing? He wanted your opinion on spirit impostors and poltergeists. Is the latter earth-bound and evil? I know you were familiar with both of these phenomena when you were in this life and did some investigation on the subject."*

**Ian:** "I did indeed do some investigating on the subject while residing in Toronto. Interestingly my research findings were not far off the mark. It is just that the picture is so much clearer here in spirit, unhampered by physical trappings and often misguided thinking. Well, to answer your question, spirit impostors basically are low entity beings, who make trouble and cause confusion. I can say with conviction, there are layabouts in this world just as there are in yours. Good and evil exists in both worlds and everything in between.

"These souls when they arrive in spirit don't come to terms

with themselves and hold the same irresponsible personalities, until deciding to correct their failings and make some progress. It is unfortunate that, at times, these impostors can manage to get through and give wrong information. This can easily happen if the psychic is not on a guarded, high-level energy link; the wrong energies i.e. impostors can infiltrate the regular communication line."

**Muriel:** *"My guide Master Chung says that the medium's guide is responsible for checking the entity's identification, because he controls the communication link between the spirit and human elements. Can you elaborate on this?"*

**Ian:** "Master Chung of course is correct. In your case, he controls your information door diligently. It also depends on the medium's level of spiritual development. Again there are exceptions and extenuating circumstances to every rule, in every walk of life. It is up to the receiver of the information to check out the source. One must always check and recheck, because this kind of information is so intangible. One should not allow the emotions to take over or rely on blind faith – the true facts are what count.

"Sometimes people try to research past lives through consultation with regular mediums or psychics. One should try several to see if the information is consistent. It would be most unfortunate to be gulled into a misconception by some spirit hoaxer taking over the psychic or others with similar energy. The most reliable source of this kind of information is through being regressed by a qualified regression practitioner –

this was my field of expertise – I guess I am a bit late for that kind of plug – eh?!

"Now you had a question about Poltergeists. These souls are actually a breed unto themselves. They arrive here in a self-perpetuated energy field, which they then project into the earth's atmosphere. This energy causes unfriendly or 'unspiritual' reactions through the physical body they choose to contact. Poltergeists are not evil in the true sense of the word, but rather they are mischievous spirits and they have to work their way out of the virulent energy surrounding them.

"The primary cause of this problematic condition is usually a build up of anger and frustration brought from their earthly existence. They try to draw attention to their plight through harassment and disruptive behaviour using the energy field of a human being. It is a very frightening experience to suddenly find an object flying through the air or a piece of furniture shifting and vibrating violently without an obvious motivator. In my physical life, I witnessed the phenomena at work during the period of my research on the subject, and it certainly was a hair-raising experience.

"These souls, filled with negativity and bad feelings would appear to be devoid of love. It is my theory that poltergeists in general, did not know love when they were on the earth and as a consequence continue to communicate with the physical world in a destructive manner in order to get the aggression out of the psyche.

"You might wonder why these souls haven't found the love that is here on the spirit side. The simple answer is – they will not accept it until they are ready. This is just one of the mysteries of the mind. These poor souls are on lower levels, if they had learned love in a previous life, they would not have arrived into that particular lower energy level.

"Okay Muriel, that's all on this subject for now. I am off with my friends to watch tennis, take care of each other. Have a nice day … bye."

## New Challenges in the World

**Bill:** It is fascinating how many of Ian's communications range across a number of topics yet help to provide the link between one topic and another. In the following conversation he reviews issues of reincarnation, of the teaching of souls, as well as bringing us new challenges in spirit communication.

**Ian:** "Hello Muriel. Say hi to Bill and Tricia. Sorry for taking so long to pick up your connection. I was taking a class of souls who are preparing to reincarnate.

"During a big gathering of our hierarchy, it was agreed that souls getting near to re-entering the earth school, would need to be fully prepared to cope with earthly problems. It will be necessary to keep focused on the need for love of humanity and the universe. Knowledge of life and what the journey is all about, will be a priority among those who are at a certain level of evolvement, and planning to return to your tumultuous planet. Their task also is to live within the laws of the universe, keep connected to the higher self and the higher power to which we are all infinitely tied – in both worlds.

"In spirit, we are committed and working towards bringing the material world into closer communion with the elements of Light, Love, Peace and Understanding; although spirit law ensures that our level of influence does not infringe on free will. This is the unique and obligatory part of our soul growth in the human being, throughout the earthly journey. We have great teachers of wisdom in the spirit realms. Souls reside here who have, in their past existences, coped and succeeded in overcoming the evil intents of their fellow men during their lifetimes.

*"It is our purpose to step up the level of spirit communications with your world.* We will impart spiritual wisdom, and spread the message of truth, by working through dedicated souls within your dimension.

"Thank you Muriel, I just had to get this message through to you while it was still 'hot off the press'. Talk again soon. Bye for now."

## Research Notes for Chapter 9

**Poltergeists**

I feel it is appropriate here to mention Camille Flammarion's (1924) book, *"Haunted Houses"*. This book described poltergeists as part of a whole class of haunting phenomena which used to be called 'rapping spirits'. These were particularly studied in Germany under the name of 'Poltergeist' ('polter' – meaning to make a commotion; 'geist' – a spirit) and were comprised of noises, raps, uproars, movements, sighs and murmurs.

Flammarion also provides a fascinating and detailed account of poltergeist activity told by a witness to a series of events in the village of Swanland, near Hull in England. The witness was a Mr. Bristow who served as an apprentice in a carpenter's shop. He related the full details of a series of events involving small pieces of wood which were thrown at the apprentice and his two companions. Each person was sure that the one inch pieces had been thrown by one of the others! Through Flammarion we can learn the conclusion of Mr Bristow's eye witness account.

*"From time to time a piece of wood just cut, would start to dance amidst the tools. It is remarkable, in spite of innumerable attempts, we could never catch a piece while it was in motion as it cleverly eluded all our stratagems. They seemed animated and intelligent. This state of affairs continued for six weeks. Sometimes it was quiet for a day or two, but then would follow days of extraordinary activity, as if they wanted to make up for the time lost. Without exception, all of these objects came from the interior of the shop. Not a single piece came through the door.*

*"One of the strangest peculiarities of the manifestation was, that the pieces of wood that fell to the ground, somehow worked their way into the corners of the shop. Despite our vigilance they were mysteriously and invisibly raised to the ceiling, from where they would fall on us.*

*"It was established, that there was no connection between the manifestations and the three of us. The other carpenters working in the shop testified that the disturbances still continued when we were absent. There was another aspect to the mystery – the missiles only moved when nobody was looking and when they were least expect-*

ed. *We were never able to determine whether the pieces began their flight invisibly, or whether they profited by a moment's distraction on our part. Sometimes the direction taken by the projectiles was a straight line, but more often it was undulating, rotary, spiral or jerky.*

*"Numerous visitors were profoundly impressed by the manifestations, but the one most struck was manager Mr. John Gray, for a particular reason. He had lost a brother who died in financial difficulties. This brother had left a son also named John Gray, who was taken into the shop as an apprentice; regrettably he died shortly after of consumption. In the district it was said that his father's creditors had not received the money due to them, and the uncle was responsible for this. Further, it was known that the last wish of the nephew had been that his uncle would pay his father's debts. The uncle did not grant the dead boy's request.*

*"I can testify personally, to the excessive fear with which the uncle was seized when the manifestations broke out. His behaviour was that of a man petrified, and I felt sure he had made personal observations on his own account of which he did not speak.*

"The manifestations stopped immediately on payment of the debt. *No tombstone had been put on the nephew's grave. The uncle hastened to accomplish this duty also; the stone is still in the Swanland cemetery and one can read there the name of John Gray, died at the age of twenty – two years, January 5th 1849."* (pp 256–259) Camille Flammarion, who had been investigating this poltergeist activity, added the following footnote:

*"We do not find in this case any intellectual manifestation, but only the projection of pieces of wood in all directions by intentional acts, with the object of attracting attention without causing harm to anyone. The eye witnesses agree in regarding them as provoked by a deceased person with the wish of attracting the attention of a living person, and inducing him to pay a debt of conscience. The end was gained.*

*This interpretation is quite admissible. It agrees with what we concluded above:*

> *(1) That invisible beings exist;*
> *(2) That they may be human beings formerly alive;*
> *(3) That they may not be very different from what they were in life.*
> *(4) The forces in action are not unconscious; they are thinking forces acting intentionally."*

(p259)

## Spirit Impostors

The question of spirit impostors is an interesting one. It brought to my mind the case of the late Joe Fisher[2] of Toronto, a journalist and researcher into reincarnation; author of many books, including "Hungry Ghosts" (1990). Joe, a personal friend of Ian Currie and ourselves, spent over four years on, what seemed to be, a 'wild goose chase', travelling half-way around the world searching for, but receiving false information from a spirit impostor, who purported to be one of his guides. There are many cases of spirit impostors; so called earthbound spirits. It is interesting that Ian also advised caution when seeking information on past lives – you need to know that the source of the information is reliable.

---

[2] It is a sad loss that journalist and paranormal researcher Joe Fisher left our planet prematurely in April 2001.

# 10

## Untimely Departures

*"Earthly laws change constantly according to material conditions and the will of the ruling majority. The spiritual laws never change; they remain constant."*

– Ian Currie

## Suicide

**Bill:** I had some questions for Ian on the matter of suicide, and what the spiritual implications of this action would be. There have been media reports of a number of mass suicides initiated through cult indoctrination, and recent research suggests that teenage suicides are on the rise, which certainly gives cause for concern. In more recent times we have been faced with the consequences of a rise in "suicide bombings". There are also ongoing debates on the ethical status of euthanasia. If someone has an incurable disease, and wishes to terminate his or her life because of unbearable suffering, what are the views from spirit on this issue?

**Muriel:** *"Well Ian, you appear to be in your spiritual robes today, what is the occasion?"*

**Ian:** "During Easter, all the stops are pulled out and we take time to show off, if you will, our achievements in spiritual progress. So here I am in my Easter bonnet!! … ha! I guess we can call our spiritual gatherings 'the wonderful world of spirit'. Throughout the book, I have touched on our various gatherings here for our spiritual knowledge. We can attend within our level any meeting, which a Master or other learned teacher may hold on a specialized subject. By the way, I confess I was eavesdropping on the conversation that you, Bill and Tricia were having at breakfast this morning; so I already know what you have lined up to ask me!!"

**Muriel:** *"You are smart this morning! So now you know the question – please continue."*

**Ian:** "Although we have freedom of choice all the way through our lifetimes in both worlds, we must understand there are laws which still must be obeyed. According to our spiritual laws, committing suicide is a hindrance to our advancement. Consequently, upon arrival, suicides have to pay the penalty within the law of reason, for making that choice.

"The person, or persons, who committed suicide, had during their lifetime taken on the responsibility for their own soul's journey. By making this choice, it prevented that soul from achieving further spiritual progress on earth. Therefore, when they decided to cop out before their natural passing time, they had not worked out their blueprint time for that particular life. When they return to spirit before their natural time, they have to deal with the situation. So folks, I can tell you, it is better to work at your material problems, keep at them; to paraphrase Sir Winston Churchill … *never give up.*

"This law applies only to those who knowingly plan their suicidal departure from the earth planet. However, a person who commits suicide who is of unsound mind through mental illness, depression etc. will come under a different category upon arrival on the spirit plane. Mental illness is completely taken into consideration under natural spirit law. Here, this particular soul is helped and guided into a clear way of thinking. There are thousands, no, *millions* of young suicides passing over to us, and instantly they arrive, they are put into an environment similar to an 'incubator,' for want of a better word, then nurtured back into their proper level of understanding.

"During this healing process, the soul and the mind are returned to correct balance. Then these souls regain their precious free will in order to progress with their journey once more. According to their choice, they can then train their minds to be strong and learn how to deal with the next journey. Readers, you have no idea just how much work is done within the realms of spiritual understanding on this side of the veil. I cannot express enough, that each individual must come to terms with the true meaning of life eternal: it encompasses everything. This is your soul journey, it is wonderful and rewarding, if you choose to make it that way. You live your life by your inner conscience; if you haven't got one, then you're in trouble.

"Higher Intelligence – God Force – Spirit Energy: these venerable attributes to the human psyche, have all been displayed by many great people who have walked the earth before, and given their lives for others. We don't only have to be religious, but believe in eternal life and live by the laws, giving love, understanding, and forgiveness. When we are in the spirit world, we soon learn this way of life."

**Bill:** In another conversation Ian again touched on the subject of suicide. He states his case quite clearly and in no uncertain terms.

**Ian:** "I must emphasize that while in the physical body, there is no point in getting *fed up* with earthly life; and deciding to enter the spirit world prematurely by your own measure instead of passing over the veil under the natural law. Committing suicide will only set you back in your spiritual progress, because you would have gone against the natural law of the Universe. We *chose* to return to the physical body through reincarnation, and of our own free will. We *chose* to travel through the earthly journey, by struggling with all the intrinsic problems and challenges of being human, to progress spiritually as a consequence of our human efforts.

"According to the spiritual law, we must continue to work through our self–allotted life, no matter what the consequences, whatever it takes. One should not say – 'I have had enough', cop out of the physical body, and arrive here by your own method. I trust I have made this quite clear."

## Euthanasia

**Ian:** "Now Bill, euthanasia is a tricky question. We have free will and it is our own life, so we have the choice to do what we want with it. But there are governing laws in both worlds, which make it really difficult to give a definitive answer.

"I feel if we decide to take our own life prematurely, and not implicate another who, by collaboration might land in trouble with earthly law, then that is our prerogative. However, this still hinders the soul's progress. We must abide by the laws. Now earthly laws change constantly, according to material conditions, and the will of the ruling majority; *the spiritual laws never change*, they remain unbending. Therefore, we break the spiritual law by taking our own life, and not allowing the wisdom of the natural law to complete its cycle. There really is not much more I can add to this discussion. It appears to be fairly cut and dried from my standpoint – talk again."

## Murder

**Ian:** "I'm not going into all of the untimely ways some of us pass on, such as accidental deaths, wars, killings, and so on. That is another part of the universal law. When the cause of suffering and death is by another's hand, those responsible will be held accountable and pay the penalty when they get here.

"Let's take for example, someone who has committed murder or some other major criminal offence. When that person passes into spirit, he or she has already darkened the conscience, the inner self, which is the soul. Consequently, the punishment is within the self; the crime committed will automatically darken the vision. Time spent in prison paying the price to society is not enough, *because the cost of wrongdoing must be paid within the soul.*

"This is where the devil and hell, has come into our thinking. Religious belief also places the burden of wrongdoing within you. A person may pray to God for forgiveness and feel that all is forgiven, or speak with religious advisors for exemption. When that person comes home to spirit, they must reconcile within the soul for forgiveness, and cannot rest until this is accomplished. After self-recrimination and judgment, however long that takes, colour, knowledge and spiritual energy are available here in abundance for those souls ready for acceptance in the spirit plane.

"With this statement I bid you farewell Muriel, thank you and take care."

## Research Notes for Chapter 10

## Euthanasia, DNR and Suicide

Ian seemed to be quite definite in his view of euthanasia from the perspective of spiritual law. However here in the physical world, there have always been on-going debates on the subject; I offer some thoughts on this issue.

We have in this age of medical science, found ways of alleviating physical pain to make it possible to live out the course of a terminal disease, with a much-reduced level of pain and discomfort. That leaves us with the question of emotional pain. Because of medical interventions, life can be extended beyond natural expectation, but not always to the benefit of the suffering patient. Death can be temporarily cheated – but so can the sufferer. The legal introduction of the *"Do not resuscitate"* (DNR) clause gives autonomy to the dying patient. That is a choice, which does not cross over the ethical boundaries, and releases all parties from guilt. The patient dies a natural death with dignity.

When you examine the process of dying from the spiritual aspect of life, then one's perspective of reality may change. Muriel, Tricia and I, know there is an afterlife: we believe we are spiritual beings inhabiting a temporary physical body. We also believe we are here in order to learn valuable lessons that living on this planet can almost certainly provide.

From this hypothesis the idea of accelerating one's own demise through human intervention, would be to deny oneself the opportunity of enduring the dying process, which might in itself bring about a profound spiritual learning experience. Any premeditated action, may in that case diminish the fulfilment of this earthly life cycle.

As Ian has pointed out quite categorically, if we choose to end our lives before the natural outcome, then we must account for those actions when we arrive back in the spirit world.

# 11

## Out-of-Body Experiences

*"An out-of-body or a near-death experience is a phenomenon of the soul/spirit body, our etheric double."*
– Ian Currie

**What is an Out-of-Body Experience?**

**Ian:** "Muriel, your turquoise light is flashing loud and clear. I am also in a clear frame of mind, ready to answer any question Bill has for me. I will of course give as full an explanation as possible. I am pleased that you are happy with my endeavours, which come from the best of my abilities, and as I currently see things. I find it a wonderful learning experience. Soul-searching and communication: they are so important for progress."

**Muriel:** *"Well Ian, we are delighted you are enjoying these communications. Bill, Tricia and myself are always eager to hear more of your interesting, revealing activities and findings from your spirit world perspective. Bill's question refers to 'out-of-body experiences,' and also the sensation of flying that some people experience during the sleep state. What can you tell us?"*

**Ian:** "Fine Muriel, interesting questions. Just let me get with it for a moment.

"Well now, there is more than one type of *'OBE,'* which is brought about by different states of mind, or perhaps I should say consciousness, as this is the primary factor; then of course there are the circumstances, which prompted the event. I can think of four scenarios that could facilitate the *'out-of-body experience.'* The first type that comes to mind is a voluntary action through transcendental meditation. The participant enters into meditation with the express purpose of elevating the consciousness to levels far above the normal frequencies of the immediate energy field.

"For example, Yogis, Gurus and other such mystics, who have trained themselves to reach the inner self and find oneness with God, practise this technique. The soul/spirit enters an altered state of consciousness, leaves the physical body and for a time travels into other realms of consciousness. It becomes connected with the cosmic energy field, which in turn brings about a feeling of complete oneness with the *whole*, and so reaches the ultimate concept of the soul: being at one with God.

"Now the second method is again usually voluntary (but not necessarily) and this probably answers your question on *'flying.'* The sensation of 'flying' is a transitory state and can still be attributed to the 'out-of-body experience'. I know there is a certain technique which one can follow that brings about this type of *'OBE'* – I believe it requires the use of willpower, imagery and some other factor, which I can't recall, to induce this phenomenon. The participant experiences a feeling of lightness as the etheric body elevates and finds itself drifting skywards, and floating over rooftops."

**Muriel:** *"Excuse me interrupting – but you just described a scene from 'Mary Poppins'!!"*

**Ian:** "Well, where do you think that idea came from?! To continue – okay you get the picture. I believe that some people who have perfected the technique can travel fast over long distances and look in on family and friends (I don't think that's a good idea!) during the out-of-body experience. Just one other point to mention here, when the spirit re-enters the body, it has been known to do so with quite a bone-shaking jolt.

"The next aspect of the 'flying' sensation is associated with sleep. People who experience this feeling are typically at a certain stage in their soul progression. This is what happens when this event occurs: the body has settled down to sleep and the mind is peaceful, as the sleep state starts to overtake the body, the person suddenly becomes aware of being in motion, and feels as though they are travelling through space. I know this because there can be a similar sensation at the start of a regression.

"So what is actually taking place is that the soul is going over to the spirit world as it normally does during sleep, but on this occasion the mind does not fully enter the sleep state, in order to participate in the transition. This is usually a learning experience, the person then becomes aware of their surroundings in the spirit world, and can relate the experience the next day. We tend to forget we are initially spirit, and return to the physical plane as a learning experience for spiritual progress. Consequently it stands to reason that the subconscious part of the mind would travel between the two worlds, while the conscious part remains dormant in sleep."

## Near-Death Experiences

"The last type of 'out-of-body experience' we can discuss occurs through a traumatic circumstance. This is the 'near-death' experience, which happens when the soul suddenly finds itself in a frightening situation. Typically this would be a life-threatening medical emergency or accident. The trauma is a shock to the nervous system, so the soul leaves the physical body and escapes into the spirit or etheric body, where it feels safe away from the pain. The soul usually remains close at hand, watching the scene unfold from a vantage point somewhere above the physical body. In other instances of 'NDE' the soul is propelled straight into the spirit world, there are accounts of reunions with loved ones, a sense of being swept through a tunnel, visions of sacred figures and many other experiences. In all of these cases there is one commonality: each one acknowledges that either they knew, or were told, 'go back it is not your time'. When the soul returns to the physical body, that person can recall every incident that took place during the catastrophe, and most report a new and enlightened perspective of life and death.

"This out-of-body, near-death, experience is a phenomenon of the soul/spirit body, our etheric double. Many scientists do not accept this analysis because the soul/spirit is intangible. As we know, the soul/spirit/mind is the only part of our physical body that cannot be accounted for by medical science. There have been many books written by those who have experienced these happenings; there is no doubt they do occur."

**Muriel:** *"Just as a matter of interest Ian, have you ever had an 'OBE' or experimented with this phenomenon?"*

**Ian:** "Well yes, I did try at one time to reach a connection into higher intelligence. My colleagues and I used to have group meetings, and tried out all sorts of advanced methods, attempting to experience a state of self–realization. I needed to familiarize myself with different forms of spiritual practice in order to help me with my research work. I spent my life researching every way possible to give me proof of an afterlife. I was convinced that life must be eternal, on account of the lives that people relived during their regressions, and as you know I documented all my findings, and also published them.

"To get back to your question: if you had asked me while I was still in the physical body, I would probably have answered 'yes.' However, having now passed over into this world, in retrospect I would say I probably had the 'impression' that my spirit left my body and entered a state of higher consciousness, but more likely it was a state of mind rather than the real thing.

"The true 'near-death experience' is much more reliable and evidential. In the first place the person involved is totally aware of having had the experience. They can remember and describe every sensation, every nuance, and every aspect of what was happening around them, despite the fact that this person was unconscious at the time. So, no I don't believe I had a true 'OBE' nor have I experienced an *'NDE.'* The only expertise I have is an *'RDE'* – a *real* death experience!! That's all I have to say on that matter."

## Dreams

**Bill:** Ian had talked a lot about our sleep state, and the various episodes that can happen during this period[1]. To round things off, I thought we should ask about dreams, and if they are connected to spirit.

**Ian:** "Dreams are a product of the mind, and as we know manifest during a certain period of our sleep. The dream state involves past memories and present conditions. This happens at a certain level of consciousness – or perhaps it's more fitting to say *unconsciousness*. The intensity of the dream, and the clarity, usually depends on the emotional state of the dreamer, prompted by distress, fear, anxiety, excitement – to name only a few. These are humanistic elements.

"Now, there are many recorded incidents of premonitions, warning of impending disasters, which have been received during sleep. In these situations, the sleeper witnesses the manifestation of a future event, which is usually disastrous in nature. This is not a dream in the classic sense, the level of consciousness is on a different vibration or wavelength from the dreamer, and is not feeding off the memory bank or the emotions. The sleeper has in fact entered a field of higher frequency, the realm of space and time where events past and future can be accessed. There are some

---

[1] The reader may also be interested in the work of Gladys Mayer (1956). She writes that: "Sleep has great spiritual significance as it is the individual's entry into the world of spirit." (p99)

psychics/mediums who can do this sort of thing naturally, without going into an altered state of consciousness.

"In summing up – I would conclude that dreams are of a physical nature, and premonitions in sleep are of a 'psychic' nature, they are quite different states of consciousness. Having said this, I realize that things are not quite as black and white as I have depicted, and there is a big grey, overlapping area between; so perhaps I am guilty of over simplifying the issue. However, for the purpose of this book, I feel it is sufficient to differentiate between the two sleep states (dream state and premonition) without getting caught up in the many diversifications. All right Muriel?"

**Muriel:** *"That sounds good to me Ian, thank you. Tell me, are you off to do something special now?"*

**Ian:** "Well actually, I am now going to gather my class together and get cracking, my regards to all, bye for now."

# 12
# The Mind and its Mysteries

*"The mysteries of the mind are concealed in past lives, and so one's previous lives relate directly to the present one. We carry our mind and soul through each incarnation."*
– Ian Currie

**Bill:** I have had a life-long interest in the mysterious workings of the mind and how we can train our minds to behave in new and different ways. However I was also keen to understand the relationship between the soul and the mind, and how this might change with each incarnation.

## The Mind

**Ian:** "Mysteries of the mind are concealed within past lives, and so one's previous lives, relate directly to the present one. It varies from person to person, depending on the individual spiritual advancement and progress. It is impossible to know, exactly what makes up the unseen mysteries of the mind. Of course, how one conducts one's present life, also bears importance in finding out where the hidden thoughts lie. Life would be easier, if we could understand our inner thoughts and their origins. Sometimes these inner thoughts can give rise to perplexing attitudes, fears, and irrational behaviour, which does not always fit with that person's present persona. That is where past lives come into play. I will elaborate more on this particular issue in a later conversation."[1]

**Muriel:** *"Thank you Ian, we will look forward to hearing more about that fascinating subject when you are ready. Meantime Bill, Tricia and I were discussing the relationship between the mind and soul; can you clarify the connection for us?"*

**Ian:** "Fair enough Muriel; the first thing to know is ... *the mind is one with the soul.* We carry our mind and soul, through each incarnation. The soul is our being, our seed. We could say it is the seed of our evolution. This is the only unseen, unidentified part of our physical body; however there are many scientific contradictions about this.

"The soul/spirit energy is connected to the God Force. The mind and soul are in unison with each other. Personality is not lumped in with the mind/soul. When the physical body dies, the personality stays with the etheric counterpart while in spirit form, but is relinquished when a new earthly life is undertaken. As I have mentioned before, at the point of reincarnation the personality is relegated to being a past life experience. Does that answer your question Muriel?"

**Muriel:** *"It does indeed Ian, thank you. Your answer was short and to the point. Is there some other subject you would like to shed light on, that might bear relevance to our conversation today?"*

---

[1] See later sections in this chapter on Multiple Personalities and Possession.

## Memory

**Ian:** "Okay, How about we talk about memory? Bill is always showing an interest in this topic.

"Memory has the same format here, as on the earth. A retentive memory on earth carries on the same way here, a short memory likewise. We already know that while in physical form, we can access some of our past lives through regression, because they are stored in that little private 'box' called the subconscious. We remember only what we want to remember, until we are regressed. When that 'box' is unlocked, we find out the hidden secrets of the psyche.

"With hypnosis, there is no interference from the conscious mind, which is the same as in regression. In the hypnotized state, all hell can be let loose in our storehouse of memories. Some memories we like; some we do not. While in spirit we can remember most of the significant stuff, we might wish to recall. I haven't checked out this statement with anyone else here, as I am talking off the cuff, so to speak. Perhaps I should say, as far as I am concerned that is how it is. However, if someone arrives into the spirit world in a condition of great anxiety and stress through physical trauma, then for sure it would take time to recover that memory. I guess you could call it 'spiritual amnesia,' the same condition that can occur in the physical body.

"We remember our lifespan of previous lives. Unfortunately, we cannot see all those lives instantly when here – certainly not on my level. I have spoken with some others who also agree, that we only retain the memories of our last lifetime, and keep them until reincarnating again. We do eventually drop details of memories which have become inconsequential. It is my understanding that as we progress into the higher planes and levels, we can recall all of our history, having reached a much higher point of spirituality. This is in accordance with the spiritual laws.

"My belief is that once our soul reaches the higher echelon, we can view the whole life path. As yet, I have been unable to confirm this. However I am assured that I will progress into a level where this will be within my scope of understanding.

"Next time we meet Muriel, I would like to talk about the personality and the subject of multi personalities, and give a 'spirit world' point of view on this issue. I have quite a different perspective from here."

**Muriel:** *"Thank you – that will be most interesting Ian."*

## Personality

**Ian:** "We talked last time about the mind and soul, being as one, and I stated that the personality was not an integral part of this union. The reason for this is quite simple; when the physical body dies, the personality stays with the etheric counterpart, but is *relinquished* when a new earthly life is undertaken. I think I have made the point before but it is worth repeating: the previous personality, at the point of reincarnation, becomes a past life memory.

"Personality is usually developed at a young age. I think it is established around the age of seven approximately. If there is a personality change through ill-health or through some traumatic experience on the earth plane, it only affects the brain, which may reflect in the mind. This condition could last until death, because the imbalance is physical. When the soul returns home to spirit from that lifetime, the imbalance will be removed and that soul will return to its intended personality. In other words, if a physical abnormality changes the personality, the abnormality or affliction is erased when we become spirit again, and we are free of any ills in the mind/soul.

"There are souls who have a really bad experience in their life, and I'm not referring here to a problem of mental health; it could be a case of extreme cruelty, or perhaps excessive hardship. It is possible that due to the traumatic nature of these events, these souls do not come to terms with that life and continue to harbour the injustices that were sustained, despite attempts to let go. As a consequence, when they return to the next material existence, this experience could resurface in some other form. The soul must eventually work through this condition in order to achieve success.

"Sometimes this mishap shows up during regression sessions, the person can then understand the origin of the feelings they experience, and are able to correct the thinking and move on. As you are aware regression work was one of my specialties while working on earth; so I can verify this at first hand. Mind you, it is also possible that these ill-personality defects may not be successfully overcome; that soul may be unable to let go, and as a consequence cannot progress spiritually. Therefore that experience stays locked up within the person until the situation is rectified. When this happens the soul becomes free to continue its journey. These people got lost along the way and must return to their spiritual path."

## Multiple Personalities

**Muriel:** *"Okay Ian, Bill has a question for you on multiple personalities. Do human beings who pass over, who have multiple personalities, retain them in the ethereal world and if so for how long?"*

**Ian:** "We cross over the veil in whatever shape we are in at the point of physical death. Help and guidance waits here to return us to a healthy state of being, and so the mind is healed from the effects of all bodily pain. But the personality stays the same, meaning the inner self stays intact. So to answer the 'multiple personalities' question: the problem would be in the persona, and should be healed just as any other illness is taken care of here. Then you would proceed through your spiritual path and into your level, ready to grow and make your way the same as any other soul.

"Having said that Muriel, I'm sure Bill would like to have some more information on this subject, and actually so would I. So I'll close for now and get back to you with more insight soon … Bye."

**Bill:** A few days later, Ian returned. He actually beamed in on Muriel as she woke up in bed. He had garnered more information on multiple personalities, and could not wait to share this with us.

**Ian:** "Hello Muriel, sorry for the intrusion, let's talk again on multiple personalities. It seems there are exceptions to every rule even in the spirit world. Apparently, upon arrival here by their own evolution, these troubled souls have 'dark areas' within the psyche. It can be quite an ordeal for these unfortunate souls to discard the personalities that have somehow been carried through previous lifetimes.

"After my last talk with you, I consulted with several spirit doctors and also a professor on the subject. It was agreed, many people while in the physical body have this multi-personality problem, but in a mild form. Of course the more extreme cases draw attention to the condition.

"Multi-personalities can be formulated in several different ways. There can be a malfunction of the brain causing a disease, which in turn affects the mind and initiates the illusion of imaginary beings within the psyche. The condition can also be created through fear, as a way of drawing attention away from their inability to cope with life situations. Unfortunately they lose control of their thinking and the equilibrium goes all to hell.

"Another possible cause could be that the reincarnating soul had a very strong personality during its previous life. At this juncture, that personality should be relinquished and replaced by the new one which belongs to the life just beginning. Now here comes the catch! An abnormality is created because the soul has been unable to let go of that previous dominant personality, and so carries it into its new life. The result is that two separate personalities oppose each other, which this poor soul has to cope with. Sometimes in these cases it is possible to release the previous personality through the process of regression."

## Possession

**Muriel:** *"Ian, we know there is a difference between multi-personalities and possession. Would you explain exactly how they differ?"*

**Ian:** "Possession is caused by a spirit entity taking over the mind of a person at a time of vulnerability. It could be due to a state of disturbance, severe depression or being exposed to the energy of the entity without sufficient protection. Whatever the circumstances are, the invader can get through and penetrate the energy system of this unsuspecting human being. These entities are often from an evil source, earthbound and usually full of anger and seeking vengeance. Children too can be eclipsed by these low level beings. A child, who displays unnatural, cruel and vindictive tendencies towards others, may have fallen victim to this phenomenon. Fortunately these occurrences are extremely rare.

"This invasion of the psyche obviously causes a malfunction between the mind and the brain. This comes about because there has been a complete transformation in the character of the human being, whether young or old, and the brain has to respond to a different set of commands. Now I am not suggesting that every wrong-doing in the physical plane can be blamed on some spirit entity taking over a human being. Like everything else in life, the human body can have imperfections in its system, defects in the organs, senses and so on. The brain is not always a perfect running instrument in its signals to the body.

"So in summary: we have established that possession is the intrusion of a low level entity, which wilfully takes over the personality of an unsuspecting victim, and proceeds to control that person's life in the most frightening and bizarre manner. These entities do not leave by choice: they require exorcising, or coercing into vacating the besieged victim's psyche. This is done either through the influence of a religious authority or an experienced medium; sometimes it requires both elements working together to oust the spirit invader.

"Multiple personalities are formed through malfunctions occurring within the person's own psyche. I know there are other possible explanations including medical ones. However we are primarily interested here in the soul/spirit aspect of these conditions and how they affect the human being.

"Within the scientific field of mind/brain abnormalities, there still remains controversy and doubt as to the validity of the phenomena, as I have depicted. I do believe that science is looking into the factors of the mind/soul/spirit connection in relation to the human body, and is attempting to extrapolate data in this area. Research has come a long way in the last ten years or so, due mainly to the work of inspired individuals in the field, who choose to look beyond the five senses, and make the connection between the body and the spirit.

"Well I think its time to close on this rather depressing topic, although we hardly scratched the surface. It is an extremely diverse subject – your line was very clear today. So thank you Muriel, I fancy some lunch, care to join me?"

**Muriel:** *"Thanks Ian, I decline for now. But some time in the far distant future when I don't have so far to travel, I'll take you up on the invitation. By the way what's for lunch?"*

**Ian:** "My favourite – smoked salmon!!! Bye for now."

**Bill:** The following communication with Ian came about after a sitting Muriel had with a client. She realized her client was not grounded, and the energy, which exuded from this person, was uncontrolled and abnormal. The energy in fact became so vociferous, it blocked Muriel's own channel. Muriel was concerned, and decided to consult with Ian on the matter. Here is what Ian had to say about the situation.

**Ian:** "Hi there Muriel, wonderful to be able to say hello again.

"Now your client is bordering on self-inflicted multiple personality syndrome. She is living in her imagination – all different types of lives – her energy is way off balance because she is escaping from a normal life. She has found solace in practicing dark rituals, which bring her a sense of power and control, simply because she has none in her real life circumstances. This young woman truly believes she is being spiritually guided. She captures the attention of others by talking about divine guidance and displaying strong psychic vibrations, which come from a very low level of spirit entity or entities (there could easily be more than one). It would be advisable for her to seek professional help, otherwise she will get worse and totally go into the world that she has created. Muriel, I suggest you try to warn her of the pitfalls she will encounter if she continues on this path.

"True spiritual guidance would never allow this dysfunction in her mind, or let anyone get wrapped up in phantom visions of spiritual awareness. She has an 'earthy' energy mixed with a mind which has run out of control; it takes off at any time, and enters a world of fantasy. In my opinion this is a case for a psychotherapist to handle. Adam[2] would be the man to get her out of this cycle. Okay Muriel, best of luck!"

## The Blue Planet

**Muriel:** *"Ian, after Bill had delivered a lecture in which he mentioned your name, and of course the book in progress, someone who knew you approached him, apparently she had a regression through you. She mentioned that, when still with us, you were considering writing another book, which would include an analysis of the 'Blue Planet' where it seemed she lived in a previous life. This is intriguing Ian; Bill wants to know about this 'Blue Planet' – do you remember?"*

**Ian:** "Hi there, yes as a matter of fact I do remember that – I may have had a fuzzy brain over the last few years of my life, but now that I've cleared away all the baggage I was carrying –

---

[2] Dr. Adam Crabtree, a mutual friend and colleague, is a psychotherapist and author of several books exploring the workings of the mind and personality. We shared an interest in past life therapy and regression.

I'm a new 'man' with a very clear picture of my past – my mind is in good working order.

"In the future, if you cross paths with those of my acquaintance, you have my permission to let friends know that I still maintain contact occasionally. Obviously, this only applies to those with whom I had good relations!! I often let myself wander down memory lane – trying to forget some of the not so good experiences – but then who doesn't have a few of those having coped with life on earth?

"Now you want to know about the 'Blue Planet' Bill? Well to the best of my current knowledge – there is no such planet, or destination; it solely exists in the mind. As I recall a few people that I regressed came up with this planetary image during their session, and this was what intrigued me. In the interests of research I felt the need to explore the idea; unfortunately time ran out on me. So, that said, as far as my research has taken me, it appears to be a part of the mind that lies dormant in most of us, but in some it is a place in the mind they can escape to, in order to be protected from emotions of fear.

"Perhaps all of us find solace in the so-called "Blue Planet" but are unaware that we are in this protected zone, whilst trying to deal with feelings of fear and panic. That's all I have to say on that subject Bill! If I uncover any startling new information you'll be the first to know – ha! Bye."

# Research Notes for Chapter 12

## Multiple Personality and Possession

There appears to be a number of possible explanations for identifying the cause of multiple personality affliction, and also possession.

One theory put forward in *"Esoteric Healing"* by Alice Bailey, is that there can be a loose connection between the etheric body and the physical body, presumably from the time of birth. This hypothesis would allow us to rationalize, that in this condition there could be an opportunity for other entities to infiltrate the human psyche, bringing about the multi-personality affect. Ian mentioned at one point in his communication on conception, that once the connection is made between the incoming soul and the embryo, the union is protected until the birth process is complete. Perhaps it is at that point of vulnerability that something goes amiss. After all imperfection is a part of our two worlds, until we reach those rarified planes of sheer perfection and bliss (God speed the day!) as Ian points out – we can be reborn with bodily defects and discrepancies within the mind.

## The Blue Planet and the Blue Island

I recently came across a small old[3] paperback entitled *"The Blue Island: Experiences of a New Arrival beyond the Veil"* – communicated by W.T. Stead and recorded by Pardoe Woodman and Estelle Stead.

William Thomas Stead was a highly esteemed journalist, political activist and crusader for social reform. He was the confidant of many leading public figures of that day. He had extraordinary psychic gifts and founded a psychic bureau in order to demonstrate the reality of life after death. In 1893 Stead also established the quarterly journal *"Borderland"* devoted entirely to psychical subjects. W.T. Stead perished along with 1,600 other passengers on the ill-fated Titanic in 1912.

Shortly after his passing Stead communicated with his daughter

---

[3] The date of publishing is not recorded, but the book was published by The Austin Publishing Company of California, with an introductory letter from Sir Arthur Conan Doyle which is dated 1922.

Estelle through a direct voice medium and subsequently kept in regular communication with her through the automatic writing of Pardoe Woodward. In these writings Stead describes in detail what took place at the time of his passing – and low and behold he describes how all those who passed over on that fateful night were taken together to a place which he called *'The Blue Island"*. He named it so because, in his words, *"the atmosphere had a distinct blue colour to it"* and the reason they were brought to this place was to recover and rest from the trauma of the disastrous event. It was a place of tranquillity and healing. In a way it was a special rest centre or sanctuary for traumatised, bewildered souls.

In the course of my research, I remember reading about the association of colour and the planetary system. It was theorized that when we display feelings of forcefulness, anger and intense emotions we are said to be in Mars the 'red' planet; when in deep depression one is said to be in Saturn the 'dark' planet; so the 'blue' planet or 'blue island' though nameless as yet, may be the refuge where our soul 'takes cover' in times of trauma. [4]

So perhaps Ian was not far off the mark when he spoke of a place of retreat – a *'protected zone'*, away from fear and pain.

---

[4] Also see Chapter 3: Adjusting to Spirit Life.

# 13

# Spirituality and Religion

*"Spirituality is God-given to all, enabling us to eventually reach the ultimate: pure spirit. We choose how we achieve this; freedom to choose follows us through our spiritual path in both the spirit and the earth world."*
– Ian Currie

## Religion

**Muriel:** I am waiting for Ian to arrive, and now see him appear wearing, of all things, a kilt!

**Ian:** "Good morning Muriel, I recently visited Vancouver, in spirit of course. I looked in on an evening for former graduates, at my old alma mater. There were pipers and all the paraphernalia that goes with it, so I wore a kilt. My ancestors were Scottish, and I have my own tartan; sorry for making such a sloppy entrance. On this gloomy dreary day in Toronto, I thought I would cheer you up with some minor theatrics, hence the kilt: how do I look?"

**Muriel:** *"Well I must say Ian you are always full of surprises. I approve the kilt, but don't try any auditions!! It is always nice to exchange some light banter with you. On a more serious note, we were discussing the different aspects of religious belief, and spirituality in our* *world, and the problems associated with doctrine. I am sure you have some valuable insight to share with us on this question."*

**Ian:** "Indeed Muriel, I certainly have a 'loftier' point of view now on this subject; and can talk without prejudice. To start with, one cannot talk about Religion and Spirituality without first talking about Love, the essence and basic principle of all religious doctrines; and the foundation for any spiritual practice. Without this ingredient one is neither truly religious nor spiritual.

"It is incredible the amount of love that surrounds us here in the spirit world. The same love and light envelopes everyone on the earth plane; you would be amazed how light can project from the physical plane through to spirit, as more and more people become aware of this force and reach out to help others. These energies radiate outwards and link up with spirit.

"I attended a wonderful ceremony of prayer and love here for the Pope when he became ill. I witnessed the light beaming to the earth, because of the love being projected from spirit. Also, there was a similar but simpler gathering for Mother Theresa when she was ill. It is an obvious conclusion, that when these great souls return to spirit they will be on a high spiritual plane.

"Let's try to define Religion and Spirituality briefly, without dwelling on all the ramifications. Religion inculcates listening to and following the rules and guidelines of a particular denomination; living one's life practising the principles according to, and within the confines of that creed. Spirituality in and of itself has no such boundaries and is not confined or ritualistic. Religion embraces spirituality, but not all who claim to be religious practise spirituality.

"Spirituality is God-given to all, enabling us to eventually reach the ultimate: pure spirit. We choose how we achieve this; freedom to choose follows us through our spiritual path in both the spirit and the earth world. True spiritual practice has no need of organized religion in order to function in total harmony with the Divine Power, the Source. On this side of the veil when one's life is summed up in its entirety, it is the quality of one's thoughts, actions, deeds and contributions to mankind that defines spiritual progress. Religion plays a valuable collective role in the world, but as we are all aware, it is open to the mania, abuse and misinterpretation of groups and misguided individuals."

**Muriel:** *"Bill was wondering if religious beliefs and customs continue in the ethereal world. Do spiritual leaders, from different religious denominations, continue to perform their religious practices?"*

**Ian:** "First, when we pass over into the spirit world, we are here as individuals. Our soul understanding determines our current level. That level has nothing to do with our earthly job, position or religious belief. It is determined purely on spiritual deeds, actions, service to others, sacrifices, love and compassion – the list goes on – understanding our spiritual nature, and living by the spiritual laws. Yes, easier said than done in the materialistic physical world, where our attitudes are defined more by what we see, hear and touch, rather than by what we might aspire to if we allowed ourselves to rise above and see beyond the five senses.

"So to get back to the question, the answer is yes. If you were a religious leader on the earth and you wish to continue on this course, your free will allows you to do so. If you want to talk on your faith, or listen to those of another denomination, it is your prerogative, you will continue until you no longer require that religious calling. Those who lived earthly life through their faith, will probably surround themselves in the afterlife with the same symbols and treasures that sanctified their beliefs, it's just a home from home folks – if you want it that way."

## Spiritual Planes

"Bill might be interested to hear about a seminar I attended recently; the topic was the continuation of spiritual practice here in spirit. It appears that when the soul eventually reaches total spiritual evolvement, classified religion as we understand it, disseminates and becomes integrated with the Universal Whole. In the superior planes, the Hierarchy is constantly praying for the world. Universal prayer and universal intelligence govern the higher Masters of spiritual knowledge. We in the less elevated levels, can still spend time tending to community work, and continuing to grow in our awareness of spirituality, without necessarily putting it into a religious context.

"I found the seminar interesting; participants included spirit teachers of all denominations, they are always there and ready to help. I spoke at length with an Egyptian teacher who lived on the earth at the time of Ptolemy the second. He listened to the debate, and provided answers with great command.

"The question arose – Why don't we reach great heights, i.e. higher planes and levels faster than we do; since we are receiving all this wonderful information while we are resident in the spirit world?

"Answer – You each absorb knowledge proportionate to the extent of what your spiritual understanding will allow, at this point in the development of your soul. The information you receive also has to be put to use and practised in your next earthly existence along life's path.

"All wisdom sounds wonderful when we listen to the Hierarchy – it is much the same as going to hear an inspirational speaker in the physical world. While you're there listening and being inspired, you are motivated and excited. You now have the tools to implement change in your life, you have a new understanding; but the incentive to put the knowledge into practice gradually dissipates as we become absorbed again in our own reality. To get back to the original point, it is also true that the great spiritual teachers didn't reach their respective planes in five minutes either[1]. No crash courses exist in the halls of learning!"

---

[1] Ian elaborates more explicitly on the subject of planes, levels and progression in the spirit world through several conversations in Chapter 14: Levels and Planes.

**Bill:** I have long held the view that in order for Religion to serve its true purpose in our world it must pull down the barriers and remove the blinkers of entrenched outmoded and biased beliefs. Religious figures must be seen to expand their vision to embrace all peoples of the world in Love, Harmony and Tolerance. Perhaps that day is not too far away. I am gratified to hear Ian confirming my own conviction that in the spirit world our spiritual level is defined through deeds of service and compassion: actions not necessarily prompted by religious teaching.

This next communication with Ian also bears relevance to the subject under discussion. The conversation started off in a unique fashion, with a slight departure from his usual orderly routine. It seems Ian was quite intense about making his point as he explained to Muriel.

**Understanding Spirit**

>**Muriel:** Ian is present and comes straight in with conversation.
>
>**Ian:** "One must see the importance of being in tune with the Infinite, because everything in life is based on this Power of Energy. We seldom stop to consider the value and necessity of our inheritance. What is inherent is neither who we are, nor our status in physical life. It is our *inner status and location in our life's journey* that is inherent.
>
>"Many people do not really understand the integral part of spirit. Often we do not understand others. The essential part of our existence is to help our fellow travellers, and in the process develop the soul. Unless we become more accountable for the things that we do wrong in life, we will never achieve the near

perfection that we hope to find in ourselves.

"Sorry Muriel – good morning! I was so busy trying to get this information out, I just did not acknowledge your presence; but of course I knew you were there."

**Muriel:** *"Good morning to you too Ian. Yes you took me by surprise – I think I heard you before I saw you, which is unusual."*

## Fate

**Ian:** "I want to talk briefly for a moment about *Fate*. I was having a discussion with a couple of like-minded associates, and I thought our conversation was relevant and worth sharing with you.

"We agreed that fate is just another part of being in the wrong place at the wrong time, or conversely, the right place at the right time. Many people believe it is God's will, when thousands of men, women and children die in wars and world disasters, natural or otherwise. It has nothing to do with God's will: we are each responsible for our own life. The God-power, the Infinite, is not responsible for arranging our time of death.

"If we die because of an accident, that's human error. Wars are also human errors – errors in judgment, mostly caused through fanatical religious beliefs, or greed for power. Earthly natural disasters such as tornadoes, hurricanes, earthquakes, are all part of life's trials; if we happen to be in the wrong place at the time, then it's regrettable, but not the fault of God. Events appertaining to the pattern of human life have nothing to do with the God-Power. This wonderful infinite source is neither Perpetrator nor Protector of the material world.

"The God-Power or Force is our universal connection. It is the source of love, wisdom and pure spirit energy. The God-Power is our support, our source of strength in the face of disaster and trauma. In the religious context, 'He' is called Redeemer and Saviour of *the soul* – not of the physical body. Ultimately it comes back to the fact, that our own thinking controls our existence and the decisions we make on both sides of the veil – again it's free will.

"Yes, the God-source is indeed ubiquitous; our wellspring for guidance, and help to the soul through spiritual knowing, but does not exercise power over physical events. Will close now Muriel – as always, it's nice talking with you. Thanks."

## Celebrations in the Spirit World

**Bill:** Ian has explained on more than one occasion that life in spirit carries on in the form of thoughts, much as it did while on the earth. In the same way, religious traditions continue for all occasions. Celebrations of all nations are carried out in true spiritual fashion, and embrace all souls. In an earlier chapter Ian referred to his Easter celebrations, but here are Ian's impressions on some other spirit world celebrations[2].

---

[2] See Chapter 10 for references to Easter. We note that Ian only makes references to Christian religions – he speaks as he knows – people continue in the way they know.

**Ian:** "Hello there, I can't hear myself think for all the Irish folk here in spirit celebrating their St. Patrick's Day!! They will have a great party 'tonight' or perhaps I should say 'all night' which is probably more accurate. I think I'll join in, I like a party. Now I bet you're thinking – what a load of rubbish! Just wait till you people pass on to this spirit plane, when you do, you will remember my words. Of course it is never 'night' here, the light that surrounds us is wonderful, but not from the sun."

## Christmas

**Bill:** We were busy preparing for the Christmas festivities, and about to put up the tree in the family room. It seemed appropriate to ask Ian about Christmas in the spirit world at the next communication.

**Muriel:** *"Good morning Ian, I like your red sweater."*

**Ian:** "Thank you Muriel. I was just thinking I'd like to bring some children on Christmas Eve to your Christmas tree. I remember last Christmas you had a beautiful one standing at your family room window in the area where we now talk."

**Muriel:** *"That would be very nice, Ian. Actually Christmas is the subject we wanted to ask you about. How is Christmas celebrated in the spirit world?"*

**Ian:** "You don't have to miss out on anything here. The spiritual masters – *'the top brass'* – depending on their mission of service hold prayer meetings. It's a wonderful scene of splendour and colour. Anyone can attend, as the masters come down to all the different spiritual levels, bringing knowledge and love. This is a festival of universal love – all creeds and cultures participate, working together on all levels and planes with no distinction.

"However if the celebration is particularly traditional and meaningful to you, then yes, you'll have your 'Christmas tree' here and also 'Christmas dinner' with all the 'trimmings,' but most important, it is a time to share and get together with family and friends, if you want it that way. I guess it is a continuation in our minds, as we would have celebrated on earth. We all participate the way we feel, and certainly communicate with our earthly loved ones. Christmas is a time to circulate love, and we do it the best way we know how. So Bill, when you eventually arrive here you can hang up your stocking and hope for the best from Santa. Ha, ha … Ho, ho, ho!! Now that we have cleared up that question, what's next?"

## Free Will

**Bill:** If there is one expression that has been repeated most frequently throughout this book it is free will. Ian has pressed home that message in no uncertain terms in many parts of this book, but particularly in the previous conversation. In this next short communication he again emphasizes the fact that responsibility for life lies squarely in our own court.

**Muriel:** I am sitting in the meditation room waiting for Ian to arrive. He is unusually late this morning.

**Ian:** "Good morning, sorry for the hold up Muriel. I had to help with a problem concerning a soul who was still blaming himself for a happening while in the physical body; he had done his wife a great injustice. Although he paid the price when he first came here and was progressing spiritually, he often recalls this trauma about his wife, and cannot cope with it. This soul has not really come to terms with the pain that he caused his partner. We can recall memories of past life at any time, and regurgitate incidents many times; you understand how some of us still live with our conscience.

"On the earth plane many people don't understand the spiritual side of their lives, and cannot begin to develop the inner self. During a physical lifetime they remain stagnant in the area of spiritual growth until passing into the world of spirit. In this dimension spiritual education is unhampered by earthly trappings, and is available to all who desire learning; classes are held all the time. When these souls choose to return to the human form and continue on their journey, they are better-equipped to progress.

"Those who believe in life after death already understand that the purpose of our existence is to progress through life's journey, both in the afterlife and in the human element, in order to reach the level of perfection. We are scholars in both worlds. Life is a school where we go through tests of will-power and courage, and the challenges of discovering who we really are.

"There is no doubt that we each control our own destiny, and are truly responsible for our own soul. We cannot blame anyone else for our mistakes – we always have the free will to choose to go our own way, (sometimes in life it's hard to believe this statement). The Source is there for back-up and security. The inner self is always in communication with infinity."

**Repentance and Renewal**

"Most people know that if we cause harm to anyone during our lifetime, we still pay the price in spirit even if we did so on the physical level. In our quiet moments of reflection in the spirit world, we may recall these past incidents ... case in point – the account at the start of our session, and the reason for my late arrival. The conscience within the soul needs to set itself into a higher level, come to terms with, and learn the lessons that life has taught, and move on.

"This is the sort of work some of us do here, helping those souls to get beyond the last life, make amends and as I said, move on. You see, when we're in spirit, we're at home, with time to contemplate our past. We all have to deal with our own thoughts and retributions, and we do so according to our personality – aha! – remember to factor that crucial element into the equation. The soul has to deal with the up and down swings of the personality (and don't I know about that one!). However, after all that doom and gloom – the good news is – this state of affairs is temporary, or intermittent, and for the most part we bask in the light of this beautiful spirit world, create a special place for ourselves, reunite with loved ones, and start the process of renewal. So on this happier note Muriel, I'll say goodbye till next time, have a good week."

# 14
# Levels and Planes

*"Planes are the major spiritual markers of our evolution.
The levels within are the small rungs on the proverbial ladder,
which carry us slowly but surely towards the next plateau."*
– Ian Currie

## Spiritual Progress

**Bill:** Ian had mentioned in his communications on teaching[1] that he wanted to talk further about the levels and planes within the spirit world. This is very important to all aspects of spirit life, spirituality and spiritual development, and one that is not easily understood by many here on the earth plane. There are misconceptions and mixed theories on the subject, so we were very interested to hear what Ian had to say.

> **Ian:** "The line is very clear Muriel, and I feel I could chat with you all day. I want you to know that I have moved up another level in my progress – small but secure."
>
> **Muriel:** *"That's good news, congratulations."*
>
> **Ian:** "It is really exciting when one realizes one has made another grade. It engenders a feeling of upliftment within one's

---

[1] See Chapter 6: Teaching in Spirit and Chapter 7: Masters and Guides.

self, and brings about further opportunities for learning. Of course I continue teaching, which is also a plus factor in my progression. The levels I speak of are small steps forward (or upward). On the other hand you can stand still equally on this side, just the same as in your world. It comes back again to choice, free will and all that.

"I want to make it absolutely clear, as we move through each lifetime on either side of the divide; we never fall back in spiritual progress[2]. It is not a game of snakes and ladders, as children play. One can say we climb up the ladder but never revert downwards to a lower level. However, I reiterate we can certainly experience a standstill for many lifetimes and make no progress towards a higher level of awareness. Progress depends on how much we accept the knowledge given, and whether we are able to identify with it – am I going too fast for you Muriel?"

**Muriel:** *"Yes, a little bit, I haven't had a chance to sip the coffee Bill brought me. You're right; our line is really open this morning. I always like it when we can zip along providing I can write fast enough."*

**Ian:** "We have a great connection today. I guess we're both feeling good and fine-tuned. I spoke of Masters in a recent communication and Bill was asking about levels and planes, and whether Masters come down. I think I did answer the question on Masters. They do continually come down to our level to share their spiritual knowledge with us. I am on the third plane; so far I have learnt there are three higher planes where the Hierarchy

---

[2] It is important for the reader to know that Ian corrected, elaborated and qualified this statement in a later communication (see the section on 'Soul Progress' later in this chapter).

reside. Within those three planes there are levels through which the Masters must also progress, the same law applies to all planes.

"Planes are the major spiritual markers of our evolution. The levels within are the small rungs on the proverbial ladder, which carry us slowly but surely towards the next plateau. I cannot give you a clear definition of the requirements to reach another plane – that is not within my knowledge at this point in my progression. However, here is some information I managed to glean about the seventh plane.

"I have learnt from others more advanced than myself in this area, that this plane is *pure spirit,* where the *Akashic records*[3] are kept. In addition, those who have reached perfection, the 'Who's Who' of the ethereal world also reside in this dimension. I mean of course J.C., Moses, Mohammed and all the other great ones."

**Muriel:** *"Before I forget Ian, the other night Bill and I were talking about a reference in the Christian Bible:* 'In my Father's house there are many mansions.' *Does this quotation refer to the planes?"*

**Ian:** "Indeed, that is correct. The many mansions are a reference to the spirit planes and the levels of progress. When you think about that, it is quite a neat metaphor don't you think? However it is important to realise that a level or plane in the spirit world is a level of consciousness; it is not a designated place or location.

---

[3] The Akashic (or soul) records are believed to be the complete spiritual details of all our past lives, covering the soul's progress through both earthly and spiritual planes. It is thought that these are what the Christian Bible calls 'God's Book of Judgement'.

"I must say our chats make me feel close to my earthly 'home,' even though I am settled here. I am well pleased with my progress so far. On this note Muriel I will call it a day. Thanks for listening, I will talk more about planes tomorrow – bye."

## The Lower Levels

**Ian:** "Muriel, I notice it is a beautiful day with your sun shining. I have something important to share with you."

**Muriel:** *"Hello there Ian, yes it is a lovely day. What exciting news do you have for us?"*

**Ian:** "Today I will tell you how I felt during my first visit into the lower levels of the spirit world. Amazingly, I actually experienced the difference in the cosmic energies. The landscape was dull and noticeably darker, certainly lacking in the colours we have surrounding us in our upper levels. There is just no comparison between the two. In more religious terminology I suppose this would be considered *'Hell'!*

"The team I went with was well versed in spiritual development, and equipped to help and guide these unfortunates onto a more spiritual path. I found it incredible that several souls I talked to and tried to help, said they seemed to have been there forever. I don't believe they had. I think they were just stuck in their own apathy.

"According to the laws, every soul regardless of level can avail themselves of the help, which is always just a thought away. These spiritually undernourished souls can also choose to reincarnate without receiving the benefit of spiritual counselling. Free will allows this to happen; it is still a part of the soul journey. However one imagines it, this would be a journey fraught with many challenges and all sorts of obstacles to overcome, in order to make some progress.

"I found my excursion quite a sobering experience. Although I was cloaked and protected from the low vibrations of that level, I must admit that the impressions of the heavy dark atmosphere stayed with me for a while until I was able to shake off the feelings. I distracted myself with music, good company and a few 'beverages' ha!"

**Muriel:** *"That was quite an experience Ian. I guess you won't be repeating that excursion for some time – if ever. Thank you for telling us about it. I look forward to meeting with you tomorrow."*

**Bill:** Ian's escapade to the lower levels reminds me that here on the earth, there are groups of dedicated people, who gather together for the sole purpose of projecting empathy and love into the lower levels that Professor Currie witnessed. It is a sad reflection on the human condition that degradation is still a very real part of our existence.

## Akashic Records

**Muriel:** *"Bill wants to know for the readers, if there is any more information about the Akashic records?"*

**Ian:** "Bill, I know you are dying to find out at what point you can get into the well-guarded information centre. Ah, ha, I just realized I said you were 'dying' to find out – excuse the unintentional pun Bill. All I know is when we reach a certain climax of spiritual progress, we receive automatic permission to see our past and present in a truly spiritual light.

"Let's see if I can explain the laws of our world here a little better. We are all striving to reach perfection. This can be quick or slow, depending on our life's progress on both sides of the veil, for an unspecified time. In each lifetime we keep trying to improve ourselves, re-incarnating over and over again, climbing through the levels and planes during each stay in the spirit world. As the readers have learned, we are spirit, going into the physical body on the earth plane to make our progress and then return to spirit and continually recycling.

"This is a known fact, proven by many philosophers, who in much earlier times were pioneers in the teaching of eternal life. We work our way climbing to different levels and when we reach another landmark in our spiritual growth, we eventually advance into the next plane, until we hit the jackpot so to speak.

"Muriel, I am signing off for now. I just love talking with you. Tell Bill to take it easy and not get uptight with putting the world right. His heart is set on helping people as much as he can. I know he helped me when I was ill ... bye for now."

## Soul Progress

**Bill:** Throughout the communications Ian had made references to the soul's progression through the spiritual levels and planes. Towards the end of the communications we wanted to clarify this and to understand how the soul's progress could be affected by reincarnation. The following two communications are an example of Ian's attention to detail and his concern to ensure that the information he gave us was correct.

**Muriel:** *"Can we extend the question about soul progress please Ian? When for instance a soul comes from a good spiritual level – reincarnates, and while in this lifetime has difficulty coping with life problems – can this soul deteriorate from a good person to an evil one, without the soul over-riding the personality?"*

**Ian:** "Okay Muriel let's dissect this. We are talking about a soul that has reached a fairly high level of spirituality. This soul has reincarnated, but finds the life 'he' has chosen pretty difficult to cope with. Temptations have come before him in all sorts of ways, and the will is constantly being tested. He will automatically know within himself, the path he must pursue regardless of outcome, because of the level of spiritual understanding, which this soul has attained. He will not allow himself to fall into the wrong path.

"Unfortunately we also have to cope with the genes inherited from parents, and perhaps inherited weaknesses of character. When these problems or temptations arise, the inbuilt DNA comes into play. This all adds up to measure the actions that you take to succeed in keeping your soul within the level of your last spirit life. This is when he will find out how strong his soul consciousness really is, and that is part of the challenge of human existence. Only on the earth plane can the soul experience the challenges and adversities of situations and relationships, which bring about ultimate spiritual perfection. It is through the choices we make on the earthly path that our spiritual level is determined, and spiritual credits accrued.

"The purpose of each earthly journey is to feed the soul with all the love and compassion we can muster, to strengthen the spirit in order to carry on to the next stage of evolvement. The personality and the ego are the tools we use in the physical body; they are the outward representation of ourselves to each other and the world at large. Conflict, discomfort and disease in the body and mind are due to disparity between the soul and the personality. The more closely the personality and soul are harmonised the more radiant, loving and peaceful the being becomes.

"Muriel, my answer is that every soul is unique. I cannot totally summarize behaviour simply because of all the elements the soul has to accomplish in each lifetime, and the standard the soul has set for its own growth.

"I'd better let you go and have lunch Muriel. We will talk again soon – I love communicating with you."

**Bill:** The next time Muriel communicated with Ian, he made this surprising announcement.

**Ian:** "Muriel I have talked with Chung[4] and it seems that I may have missed the salient point of your last question about soul progress. There are different answers to the question. As I have

---

[4] Master Chung is Muriel's guide.

mentioned before there are many planes within our spirit world and then many levels within each plane.

"For example a soul that reincarnated from below the fourth plane of consciousness will enter into a lower level on its return to spirit if that soul resorted to a somewhat scurrilous existence during its last lifetime. This occurs because the soul is still learning by its mistakes, and has not learned to overcome bad patterns of behaviour.

"We could make an analogy by comparing the levels within the earthly education system. As relative beginners we start off in kindergarten and primary school. When we arrive in junior school, we are assumed to have outgrown infantile behaviour – but how many times have you seen your children revert back to juvenile tactics when it suits them? So at this juncture there is a certain vacillation between levels. In high school we have advanced to the next stage of development and in normal circumstances would never resort to infantile behaviour, and so on it goes right up to the highest level. So the point I am making here is that in the spirit world when a soul reaches a certain level of spiritual development, the soul on reincarnating would not succumb to a life of evil intent because of the level of spiritual integrity attained.

"When I say 'plane' or 'level,' bear in mind I refer to a scale of spiritual evolvement and natural plateaus of spiritual understanding. If you have reached the fourth plane of spiritual consciousness, you have learnt and achieved an awareness of spirit laws. A soul reincarnating from this level of understanding will bring with it all the knowledge gained through its lifetimes and so would be equipped to recognise and acknowledge the presence of evil or wrongdoing and act according to the inner wisdom.

"Now I do not mean that you can't have a drink and watch the game, and indulge in what you fancy, if you get my gist? When I mention evil I mean – Evil – I don't have to explain that.

"The sole purpose through your journey is to help your fellow beings in every way possible – phone a friend – believe me, that's what we do here. One still needs family and friends in spirit, even though we feel safe because of the source, which generates love. Remember: your thoughts, feelings and memory stay with you.

"I'll say bye for now Muriel – that's my phone ringing ha!! Talk again soon."

**Bill:** A further communication from Ian highlighted his view that present day life is gradually becoming more familiar with the notion of the soul's progress – an idea that was clearly linked to his research work while here in his earth life.

**Ian:** "Firstly, I want to say good morning to the three of you and say, so glad the book is nearing completion. You and Bill have done a great job through the years – you will soon realize that all the time-consuming preparation, compiling and editing will be worth all of your endeavours.

"I have given you a complete account of the workings in the spirit world from my level of awareness – but keep in mind that the procedure of soul evolution is governed by the natural law of the universe, from and within, whichever level your soul will exist on when you arrive here into spiritual life. I need say no more, because accomplishments of the soul, as it travels on through its spirit and physical lives, are explained throughout the book.

"It is interesting to note at least by my observations, that there are many more materialistically inclined folk now taking time to examine soul objectivity, within their human existence. I have been following this inquisitiveness, which is connected with soul progress. I perceive a new openness toward the subject of the soul and an eagerness to enter into discussion about what happens after death. It is gratifying to see that the tide is finally turning. It is also gratifying that I can now validate all that I wrote in my own research work."

## Research Notes for Chapter 14

**Soul Progression**

I have been struck by the fact that Ian's initial descriptions of the progression of the soul are so close to those which are contained in the work of Allan Kardec which was originally published in 1857.

*"When a spirit has finished with any given trial, he has learned the lesson of that trial, and never forgets it. He may remain stationary; but he never degenerates"* (p101).

Kardec also wrote of the role of 'free will' in the soul's progression. However it is Ian's second communication, correcting his earlier view of continual upward progression, which gave us a fuller and more complete picture of how the soul learns, develops and progresses.

# 15

# Final Thoughts from Ian Currie

*"There is no doubt in my mind: the Universe is beyond human thinking. It is wonderful beyond all human comprehension. I advise everyone to make the best of their earthly journey, because life is continuous."*
– **Ian Currie**

**Muriel:** Ian zoomed right in whilst I was meditating with Master Chung. He seemed excited and obviously could not wait to make communication.

**Ian:** "Good morning Muriel, I am excited about this book. I feel we should close, as we have enough information for the readers to contemplate on and decide for themselves, one way or another, *to believe or not to believe that there is life after death.* By the time this book is published, Adam would have delivered the annual Immortality lecture, and I'm sure he will be a great success. Bill has really done a splendid job by bringing the subject of life after death to the public through the University of Toronto[1].

"Oh! I can hear a dog barking again near your ravine – it brings me back to earthly life for a few seconds. I just want to

---

[1] The first annual lecture on Immortality was held at Toronto University in 1998 in partnership with the Philosophy Department. Dr Adam Crabtree gave the first lecture in this series entitled: *'Life after Death'*.

remind you, there is no set routine here, only if you wish to make one. You can have a full spirit life without a dull moment. You can extend your circle of friends providing they are in agreement of your company! You can do everything here that you did in your earthly life; only *it is all in the mind*. Remember if you want to go dancing even if you have two left feet, you just glide round the floor with your partner – ha! ha! However, although you have free will remember you are here to progress spiritually also, so one must use the time to increase spiritual status.

"Let me remind you about how I spend some of my time here in the spirit world. I travel around the universe, to universities, sitting in and listening to professors, watch tennis on the earth plane, attend seminars by various spirit scientists, and also by higher Masters that come down to my level. From time to time I meet with family and friends who are here, exactly in the same way as on the earth plane. That's only if they wish to see you of course, depending on how the relationship was while on earth. However with the spirit of love that is here, one usually tries to get a better understanding of each other and this eventually prevails.

"How wonderful it is to know that we have reached this far with the book. I sincerely hope I have been constructive with the information from my end. I have tried my best to tell you all I have gone through, and learnt about the workings of life in the spirit world, while keeping it in the simplest form of understanding. It is not the number of conversations that count, but the quality of, and accuracy of, information. I am still learning and gaining knowledge and will continue to do so, therefore gaining bonus points to escalate up the ladder to spiritual success! What I mean by this, is advancement to higher levels here in the ethereal world. It is strange how I did have a pre-conceived idea of what I would find here on arrival, but it did not come close to spirit world reality. Of course, all I have given you, the readers, is information I learned from the levels I went through during my progress and where I am now. There are obviously variations as we progress onward.

"There is no doubt in my mind, the Universe is beyond our human thinking; it is wonderful beyond all human comprehension. I advise everyone to make the best of their earthly journey, because *life is continuous*. Use this knowledge to keep going and never give up, as I did at times. It is great in both worlds, provided we listen to the inner self. Always remember that life is our soul journey with spirit energy helping all the way.

"I would like to indulge briefly in a little retrospection, if I may, concerning my last physical journey. The latter part of my abbreviated life was spent almost totally immersed in paranormal study and research. I intellectualized the subject to the maximum; in so doing I did not use the knowledge I had accumulated to the benefit or enhancement of my own life, from a spiritual perspective. I did not internalize the information and use it to nourish and expand my consciousness.

"My research work in the metaphysical field was purely an extension of my anthropological studies, an academic exercise to seek out the truth, and prove survival of the soul after death. In order to remain completely objective, and to view results without prejudice or bias, one must detach oneself from intimacy. Consequently, I never became personally involved in the spiritual aspect of the work in the sense of moving towards a more spiritually fulfilling life. Of course I left the planet rather prematurely, and I do believe that in my retirement years I would have taken the time to conceptualize my knowledge and move towards a more subjective spiritual role as indeed, having crossed over, I now truly encompass.

"I wish everyone the best on the spiritual path and may you reach all understanding of the *whole*, finding *love and peace* within yourselves. It can be a rocky road; just do not lose sight of your spiritual goal. The Big L here means **Love, Light and Life Eternal.**

"Muriel, you have been marvellous with all our chats and devoting your valuable time, in spite of your regular pressures in your daily business, to help complete this book. I thank you for being there for me, and listening and writing patiently on my down days when I first arrived here. It was hell to sort myself out; my mind was in turmoil. However, that part is over now, and I trust that I am sailing towards higher levels as time moves on. Over the years we have come to know each other through our 'spirit hot line', and I wish you every success in your spiritual ventures."

**Muriel:** *"By the way Ian, I notice you are wearing your robes today."*

**Ian:** "You do not miss anything, do you? My thanks to you Bill, for all your endeavours and research questions on the spiritual, as well as the help you gave me when I needed it on the earth plane. No doubt, when you join us in the ethereal world it will always be question time. From knowing you and watching you on many occasions, I can see it will be committee meetings, seminars, and attempting meetings with God in person, if possible, ha, ha!

"Muriel, we will see how things work out. There may be another book from me in the near future. Keep in touch please; I will be around. Just plug in if you wish to know more. May you the reader, gain many spiritual credits as you journey on your path, before reaching this beautiful ethereal world. Bye and God Bless."

# Epilogue

# The Survival of Intelligence And Personality

## INTRODUCTION

**Purpose and Method**

My purpose here in this final statement is to present a case to you, that human intelligence and personality survive after death. Now that you have read the fifteen chapters of the late Professor Ian Currie wherein he confirms positively that life continues after death, I will take this opportunity to take you back to the late 1950s to the beginning of my research for a purpose and method of finding evidence of the afterlife.

I will present this as a court case wherein you the reader will be the Judge and Jury. As of yet, we cannot produce a materialized spirit in a courtroom, maybe some day it might be possible. For the purpose of this work therefore and in the absence of physical matter as evidence it is normally accepted that there should be a volume of substantiated evidence together with corroborated witness testimony. I will therefore offer you documented and authenticated evidence from my extensive research. Additionally I will offer you my own witness testimony which has been supported by mediums and researchers in this field. Only when you have read this proof will I ask if you, as the Jury, are satisfied by the proof I have offered you.

All researchers have several rules to follow and this field of research is no different.

1. Never accept blind faith.
2. Obtain repeated similar results.
3. Read many documented similar results before acceptance.
4. Remove all boundaries of Universities, Institution, or Religion.
5. Always approach research with an open mind.

All these I tried well to follow throughout my research and investigations.

## Guiding Questions

My lifetime's research has been guided by several important questions. These have included the questions asked by Maurice Maeterlinck: *"Do all things end at death? Is there an imaginable afterlife? Whither do we go and what becomes of us? What awaits us on the other side of the frail illusion we call life? The moment when our heart stops beating, does matter triumph — or does mind? Does endless darkness or eternal light begin?"* [1]

Well, we shall see! No one escapes bodily death. A case for survival of human intelligence after physical death is the challenge! We will per-

---

[1] Maeterlinck's book *Measure of the Hours* is now out of print but this quote can be found in Nearing (1998).

ceive the continuation of human energy consciousness after physical death and not, as some in mainstream science believe that all comes to an end after death within cemetery walls or mausoleums – to eventually return to ashes and dust where mankind labours tilling the soil of the earth eventually bringing food to the table from where deceased human bodies were once buried.

I have also been guided by a more general, and ancient, question: *If a man dies – shall he live again?* This was the question asked by Job[2] as recorded in the Old Testament of The Bible. My own questions through my research have also included: *Do spiritual gifts exist? Who has used them? How have they been used?*

**Evidence**

The first part of my case to you will be the presentation of documented and authenticated evidence from over 4000 years ago right up to modern times. It will include evidence written in baked clay, in Biblical writings, history books, scientific books and psychic journals. It will include the use of psychic gifts for predictions, advice and counselling by Pharaohs, Royalty, Religious leaders and Popes, as well as by Presidents, Prime Ministers and ordinary individuals. This evidence has been garnered through fifty years of research work in the field of the paranormal.

The second part of my case will be my own personal experience as witness to a wealth of evidence of the survival of the human personality. These experiences have been supported and authenticated by well-known and well-respected mediums and psychics in this field.

---

[2] The Bible: Job Ch 14 v.14.

The third part of my evidence is the conversations presented in this book. It is my desire that these conversations may have answered the questions for some of you, or at least provided food for thought and kindled the desire for further exploration. This is therefore a 'Court Case in Writing' for you the reader to be the judge and jury to decide whether life exists after death in a spirit world and a case for or against the survival of human personality after death. Such a case has never, to my knowledge, ever been presented in this way.

**Background to my Research**

In the late 1950s I started my search for truth to discover what really happens to each of us when we die. I was a novice part-time actor in London, England and was considering a political career (you may think that actors become politicians and politicians – actors!). At the time I found myself undeniably drawn towards matters of the paranormal and a strong desire to search for the truth. I had been brought up as a Roman Catholic and had a sister who was, and still is, a Roman Catholic nun. I began studying other basic religions in search of truth. I could not believe there was only one religion claiming to be the truest according to Pope Boniface VIII in 1302. I studied the Christian Bible, the Torah of the Jewish faith, the Qur'an of the Muslim faith and the Hindu holy book, Bhagavad-Gita. I learnt that religions are generally accidents of birth and doctrines are sometimes changed over time. I also discovered a common thread running through those basic religions concerning spiritual laws: such as *'The prayer of faith will save the sick.'* – *'He who believes in me will also do the works that I do'* seems to be the prevailing message. Many material laws are changed through the years to suit the climate, but spiritual laws remain the same. I decided to term myself a *Christian freethinker*, without boundaries. Why? Because by studying the

Christian Bible I came to believe in Master Jesus the Christ and his well-documented psychic divine power. Pythagoras, the famed philosopher, once said: "Let human groups divine their own religions – but have your own". So I have, and have abided by the laws of spirituality.

## Consciousness

Before moving on to my evidence I would like to take a moment to talk about consciousness. Dr Edgar Mitchell (1996), the moon astronaut, has written extensively on this subject. On his return from space he stated. *"My view of our planet was a glimpse of divinity."* Mitchell explains how he experienced an epiphany and felt "an interconnectedness" with the Universe. In an effort to better understand his experience he turned his attention to the exploration of the larger related questions about the basic nature of this "consciousness." In his book he states. *"The most neglected fields of consciousness studies lay in the realms of the mysterious states of mind that allow for epiphany and the psychic event."* He goes on to say *"I knew there was something worthy of serious investigation if the issue was approached in a manner different from the traditional."* Mitchell did indeed carry out extensive research on the paranormal and conducted all manner of scientific testing. He gives a clear account of his findings in this most absorbing book[3].

Occasionally humankind can voluntarily extend consciousness beyond the limitations of the five-sense physical anatomy and explore in the fourth dimension by developing their paranormal sixth sense. It could be said that mankind, to all intents and purposes, is a spiritual facsimile of the Infinite creative intelligence, the Fountain Head, or the Cosmic Mind, in whatever manner and way this Infinite intelligence can

---
[3] See Mitchell and Williams (1966) Ch 10 p65.

be comprehended. Through evolution, mankind can gain a clearer understanding of the spirit nature of 'self', through life experiences in the astral or fourth dimension and in the material of the third dimension. The Spirit or the higher energy of mankind is the nucleus of an expanding Consciousness.

Therefore mankind is not wholly physical even though men and women appear to be a physical representation in an atomic form. It is our prerogative, and some may say our duty, to extend our consciousness beyond the limitations of the five senses and expand into the sixth sense. It is well documented in The Bible and other Holy books that mankind has continued to develop these spiritual gifts. The Apostle Paul wrote about spiritual gifts that were handed down to mankind and Jesus of Nazareth, when questioned about his miracles of healing, is recorded as replying: *"He who believes in me will also do the works that I do, and greater works than these will he do."*[4] We will explore further how many references there have been to both spiritual gifts and to life after death in countless documents both before and after The Bible was written over two thousand years ago. *Spiritual gifts* are still alive today and *mediums and psychics are stronger than ever.*

---

[4] The Bible: Corinthians I Ch 1 v.1–12.

# DOCUMENTED EVIDENCE

## The Twelve Tablets at Ninevah

I would like to highlight at this point that research on spirit communication sometimes assumes that investigation into the paranormal is a relatively contemporary phenomenon. Not so, according to author and past editor of the *Psychic News,* Fred Archer (1966), who writes that in the findings in the ruins of Nineveh there were twelve tablets written in cuneiform characters on baked clay which have been dated to approximately 4000 years ago. These tablets describe a spirit communication at a séance, relating to "the Babylonian Story of the Flood and The Epic of Gilgamish".

## The Old Testament

The Old Testament of The Bible describes, in the book of Samuel[5], how King Saul, in disguise, visited the Witch of Endor, and spoke with the spirit of Samuel. We also learn of Moses having many spirit visitations – the most well-known of which is that of a spirit voice speaking out of a burning bush, stating that he should approach the Pharaoh and ask to take the Israelites out of Egypt.

## The New Testament

In the New Testament there are countless examples of spirit visitations, psychic gifts, healings and the use of psychic powers by Jesus Christ, as well as his disciples and followers. These spiritual gifts have been practised and documented in the Bible. In the Epistles of Paul

---

[5] The Bible: Samuel I Ch 28 v.7–25.

you will find many references to all the spiritual gifts that mankind has been given: wisdom, healing and miracles, as well as spirit manifestations. Additionally Cerutti (1977) in her biography of Olga Worrell provides a definitive classification of psychic gifts, manifestations, healing and much more. She identifies and then classifies some 114 miracles performed by mediums and psychics and which are described in both the Old and New Testament. This is impressive evidence of the spiritual gifts endowed on individuals both before and after the teachings of Jesus Christ and his display of psychic gifts. The practice of Christianity strengthened over time with the Apostles and Disciples preaching about these spiritual gifts bestowed on mankind for its benefit, with seers and seeresses playing their part with prophetic messages in churches.

**Prophecies and Messengers for Popes and Clerics**

Moving away from the evidence in The Bible, one can find further documented evidence gathered by Catherine St-Pierre (1994). She writes how Thomas Aquinas (1225–1274) had taught that men have always been gifted with the spirit of prophecy given direct from God. She further reports how Joan of Arc (1412–1431) was condemned by an ecclesiastical tribunal as a heretic apostate and was burned alive at a public square and condemned as a witch. Joan's prophecies and "voices", though accepted by Royalty, were condemned by the Church and considered as acts of the devil. It took hundreds of years before she was canonized and exonerated and eventually viewed as a heroine and a martyr.

According to Fred Archer (1966) the psychic gifts of clairvoyance, clairaudience and trance sittings were practised in Church services by mediums and psychics who were, at that time, known as seers and seeresses. Archer provides evidence to us that these spirit communications were undertaken from as far back as A.D. 140.

Catherine St Pierre additionally writes of the role played by seeresses in foretelling the future for many popes. Catherine of Siena (1347–1380), who was also called "Joan of Arc of the Papacy", enjoyed great authority in the Church in her time, due to revelations she received for the Papacy during the years of turmoil. She gave direction to Pope Gregory XI in Avignon, urging him strongly to bring the Papacy back to Rome and did succeed in persuading him to return to Rome. There were other seeresses like Saint Hildegard (1098–1178) who was proclaimed as the Great Prophetess of the New Testament by the Papacy as a result of the high number of miracles performed.

Another woman of great prophetic talent was Anna Maria Taigi (1769–1837) who also influenced the Church through her extraordinary prophecies for forty-seven years. One of her biographers was Cardinal Salotti and he bears witness to *"the great influence she exercised on the supreme direction of the Church by reading the past, present, and future for the Papacy"*[6]. The humble woman, Anna Maria Taigi, had succeeded in pleasing the papacy through the volume of her accurate evidence.

Seeresses continued their work of miracles and prophecies as servants of God and the Church. Through the work of Theresa of Avila, Pope Gregory XVII sanctioned that women should be ordained as priests. However, as time went on, the work of the seeresses became quite openly denigrated and they were persecuted by St Jerome of the Papacy, who issued a decree abolishing the use of psychic gifts, despite this being against the teachings of Paul and the words of Jesus. The

---

[6] As quoted in Catherine St Pierre (1994) p29.

1765 Witchcraft Act was also used to persecute many women who possessed powers of healing or prophecy and continued to be used to persecute them right up until the twentieth century.

## Evidence from the Nineteenth and Early Twentieth Centuries

Despite the persecutions there were still people who continued to discover, practice, and develop their psychic gifts. The most prominent and publicly documented of these was in New York, USA in 1849 with the discovery of the Fox sisters, Kate and Margaret who publicly demonstrated their psychic gifts. They were able to demonstrate spirit table turning and rapping and such like. This soon spread throughout the Continents, whereby psychics and mediums (as they were now being called) were gaining world prominence in their exposition of psychic gifts.

The first Spiritualist Church was recognised in 1853 and The American and British Societies of Psychical Research were set up in the latter part of the nineteenth century. Professor William James of Harvard University was one of the Founder members of the Psychical Research Society. In 1886 during the course of his research James discovered the work of the great psychic Mrs Piper, which inspired him to write of her prowess. He reports and documents how she delivered valuable information through her spirit guide, Dr Phinuit. Professor James wrote two volumes on human personality and its survival[7]. He was also a close friend of the great F.W.H. Myers (1843–1901) who was a philosopher, a pioneer of psychical research, a Rhodes Scholar, and a poet.

Another celebrated researcher was Sir William Crookes, elected a Fellow of the Royal Society in 1863. Crookes was noted for his exper-

---

[7] See bibliography for details of works by James. Also see Murphy and Ballou (1960).

iments with medium Florence Cook who produced a materialised spirit, Katie King. This was reported in the British psychical research journals. Crookes also worked with the world famous Daniel Douglas Home (1833–86), whose experiments in levitation and materialisation are well known to many. One experiment of particular note was that of the spirit hand of Napoleon which, during the materialisation, signed an autograph on a piece of paper – the signature was later verified as authentic and belonging to Napoleon. Home was himself seen levitating by an independent reporter who witnessed him floating out of a window in a London street – this, as you might imagine, attracted much media attention. These events and many others are documented in Smythe and Stemman (1991).

Sir Oliver Lodge (1851–1940), Fellow of the Royal Society, famous scientist, and inventor of the Lodge spark plug for cars was also a famous paranormal researcher. The late Oliver Lodge, author of many books in his lifetime, communicated through psychic Malcolm Smith in Gibralter, with a team of spirit scientists, including Franz Anton Mesmer (1734–1815). These communications have been documented by Smith in his (1995) book: *"Nobody Wants to Listen – And Yet!*

In 1926 the Society for Psychical Research organised a public Symposium "The case for and against Psychical Belief" held at Clark University, Massachusetts, USA to decide on the evidence *'for and against psychical belief'*[8]. A total of 14 professors and researchers attended, including Sir Oliver Lodge, Sir Arthur Conan Doyle, Gardener Murphy, Hans Driesch, Harry Houdini, Joseph Jastrow, and more. Each speaker gave evidence, using protoplasm–ectoplasm[9] as a work-

---

[8] See Murchison (1927).
[9] There is an explanation of the term *ectoplasm* in the Research Notes on p172.

ing hypothesis. The symposium members voted on the evidence and the results were: 10 For; 2 Against; and 2 Undecided. The symposium is perceived to be a positive endorsement of psychic phenomena by the greatest psychic researchers of its day.

## Twentieth Century Evidence of Priests, Political Leaders, Police and Doctors

There were many other documented writings by paranormal researchers, but there were also documented accounts of manifestations and psychic gifts of priests and spiritual leaders in the twentieth century. Monsignor Hugh Robert Benson, son of a former Archbishop of Canterbury in England, was a psychic when he was alive. His works were claimed by others to be from the devil. He had many spirit communications with his friend Anthony Borgia which are documented in Borgia's (1954) work. In one such communication he stated that religion had taught him very little of the spirit world, that there was no such place as Heaven or Hell, and that there had been no Judgement scene. He further stated that he still had an ethereal body and mind with soul and spirit. Interestingly this account is similar to that of Sir Oliver Lodge and those communicated earlier in this book.

One of the most important contemporary events in the development of mediumship and investigations into spiritualism was the repeal of the Witchcraft Act and the introduction of the Fraudulent Mediums Act in 1951. It was widely believed that Winston Churchill had consulted with psychics in wartime Britain and had therefore been concerned about the use of the Witchcraft Act in prosecuting Helen Duncan for her communications with the spirits of sailors who had been killed on ships which the Government had not yet reported as being involved in certain battles in World War II.[10] The Fraudulent Mediums Act made it legal to demonstrate psychic gifts or mediumship, while making it illegal to claim powers which did not exist. Like others, I believe that Churchill's support for this new Act was an example of his belief in the use of psychic gifts, as well as further evidence of these gifts by world leaders. This Act is generally viewed to be a momentous step forward in allowing spiritual gifts to be exercised once again in churches and public places.

There have been other modern world leaders who also believed in the existence of psychic gifts. It is well known, for example, that President Abraham Lincoln[11] was a believer in spiritual gifts, and that his wife was a gifted medium. It is also widely believed that Past Presidents have consulted with psychics. The late Canadian Prime Minister, Mackenzie King, was a spiritualist who conferred with the spirit of the late President Roosevelt – this has been documented and confirmed.[12] A New York media correspondent, Percy J Philip, has given sworn testimony that Mackenzie King appeared to him on a park bench near Kingsmere, Quebec, four years after his death. This became world media news.

There is evidence of the use of psychics by the Police in many parts of the world, with some very positive results. Some of you may have been sceptical about the results of the more sensational media stories in the popular press, however one case is particularly worthy of note: the murder of parapsychologist D Scott Rogo, who had written many books on the paranormal[13]. The Los Angeles Police Department

---

[10] *Psychic News* February 19th 2005.
[11] *Psychic News*, November 6th 2004.
[12] See Colombo (undated) pp169–173.
[13] See bibliography.

according to a CBC radio extract brought in six psychics to solve this murder case, under Deputy District Attorney Andrew Flier. Eventually the spirit of Scott Rogo was contacted and he helped to solve his own murder. He pointed out an oversight by the Police who had not examined a wine glass for fingerprints. On the basis of this evidence gained by information from a spirit source, one of the assailants was eventually convicted and sentenced to fifteen years in prison.

Medical doctors have also produced documentary evidence of contact with departed relatives or of 'Out-of-Body' experiences. In an earlier chapter I have referred the reader to the work of Dr Elizabeth Kubler Ross (1974) and Dr Raymond Moody (1975) who did extensive research with dying patients who were able to make contact with departed relatives. Additionally I have previously mentioned the research by Dr Kenneth Ring (1998) that demonstrated how people who have been blind from birth can see while having a Near-Death or Out-of-Body experience. The reader may be familiar with the work of Professor Charles Tart (1997), also the author of over fifteen books and papers on Parapsychology, who explains the case of Pam Reynolds and her 'Out of Body' experience during her operation. Pam Reynolds had an eight hour operation for a brain aneurism. A drug was used to block any memory experience of the pain and the surgeons systematically shut down her bodily functions, which included stopping her heart and flattening her brain waves.

In Pam Reynolds' own words she had 'the most wonderful OBE, while in a temporary state of death'. She explained later to the surgeons all that she had observed in great detail. How do we explain this? If you believe the mind and the brain are one, then you will have some difficulty understanding Pam Reynolds' testimony. If you believe, as I do, the mind is connected to the soul, then this account bears perfect witness to that premise.

## Contemporary Psychics

There have been a number of well-researched psychics in contemporary times: Thomas Sugrue (1942) for example, has documented the work of Edgar Cayce in *"There is a River"*; the work of Lady Gladys Osborne Leonard (1931) is described in: *"My Life in Two Worlds"*; and the famous Jane Roberts' psychic gifts are documented in her (1970) work: *"The Seth Material"*. Many will have heard too of Rosemary Brown, a psychic who hardly knew music. However in 1971 she wrote *"Unfinished Symphonies"* through spirit communication over several years with famous composers, such as Liszt, Beethoven, Chopin, and others. She too was well scrutinised, but the manuscripts were authenticated by musical experts. I would also like to refer you to two other impressive pieces of documented evidence, both by Ruth Mattson Taylor. She worked with British clairvoyant Margaret Flavell who had conversations with Rev A.D. Mattson, the author's late father. *"Witness from Beyond"* (1975) and *"Evidence from Beyond"* (1999) both add to the volume of evidence for my case of survival of human personality and intelligence.

In more modern times there has been the work of American psychic James Van Praagh who, when performing in public, has been proved to be correct 97% of the time. I saw Van Praagh a few years ago when he came to Toronto. He was very impressive and gave me an excellent confirmation of my life's path. Television has also played its part in spreading knowledge and information about psychic phenomena. The popular psychic, John Edwards now has his own regular TV programme, called 'Crossing Over'. Millions of people have seen evidence of psychic gifts and of the survival of their loved ones through the messages he transmits to them[14].

My documentary evidence is almost coming to a close. I have shown how psychic gifts have been demonstrated by many, and used from ancient times to modern times by Pharaohs, political leaders, religious leaders, police, and ordinary individuals. Such events have been documented by scribes, historians, scientific and psychic researchers. I have referred to authenticated evidence and documented accounts of extraordinary spiritual powers and gifts, the evidence and documentation of scientists and the involvement of spirit scientists. I have cited mostly evidence which has been substantiated and replicated on many occasions by psychic researchers across the world and throughout recorded time.

## The Scole Experiments

Any contemporary review of the evidence would not be complete, however, without referring to what have been called the Scole Experiments. These took place in the 1990s in a small town called 'Scole' in Norfolk, England.

A small group of people recorded wonderful results of materialisations of hands, faces, apports, messages on tape, and photos appearing on unopened sealed spools of film. Robin P. Foy was one of the principal sitters with his wife Sandra in the Scole Group and who set up both the *Spiritual Scientist* Magazine and the Noah's Ark Society. Sadly both these have now been dissolved. The Scole Group meetings led to visits from members of the Society for Psychical Research (SPR). David Fontana,

---

[14] See bibliography for references to the works of these psychics.

Arthur Ellis and Monty Keen were witnesses to the phenomena and documented evidence for the Society. These experiments were clearly replicated on several occasions with scientific and psychical researchers being present to observe the results. I would like to pay tribute to Robin Foy whom I came to know personally through his work on the Scole Experiment. Robin works tirelessly with great integrity and enthusiasm to further the development of mediumship and physical phenomena in the interest of Spiritual Science. Robin's (1996) book *"In Pursuit of Physical Mediumship"* is a testament to his philosophy.

Additional proof and authentication was sought by scientists from NASA, professors from the Institute of Noetic Sciences (IONS), and from Stanford University, who arranged a further meeting at a venue kept secret from the Scole researchers who were flown over to the States for the occasion. This meeting took place on a Californian mountain which was subsequently discovered to be a sacred American Indian site, although this fact was not known by the researchers. The séance which took place was very positive and included loud sounds from the spirit of a native Indian chanting and dancing to the beating of drums high on a wall above the scientists seated below. Once again the experiments that took place in Scole were replicated in California with a new team of scientific observers. A positive detailed report of all these experiments is now published in journals and books[15]. The SPR (1999) Report contains an independent observer's positive report from Dr Crawford Knox who states: *"It is likely this experiment will mark an important step in attempts to place on a firm footing, evidence for the existence of a spirit world, its impact on our everyday world, and for survival after death."*

I have brought to you a few examples from my extensive library of

---

[15] See for example Solomon (1999) and *Proc of the SPR* (1999) Vol. 58.

documented evidence which exists to support my case for the survival of human intelligence, for the existence of an afterlife, and for the existence of psychic gifts. Before leaving this section I would like to draw attention to the less well-known phenomena EVP (Electronic Voice Phenomena) and ITC (Instrumental Transcommunication). This manner of communication comes in the form of discarnate voices 'transmitting' directly through electronic instruments i.e. audio electronic tape recorder, wireless, television and even the telephone as opposed to communicating directly through a human channel. There is some intriguing documentation on the subject which was detailed by David Fontana (1992) in an article "Electronic Voice Phenomena Re-visited."[16] In his article he explores the work of Dr. Konstantin Raudive (1971) and the more recent work of Samuel C.R. Alsop (1989). Another researcher in this field of study is Mark Macy whose work, in collaboration with Dr. Pat Kubis (1995) is an interesting read and provides much detail about his many experiments and findings. I found out quite recently that the Scole group in Norfolk England (referred to earlier) have now restarted and are conducting experiments in EVP and ITC – I look forward to hearing of their results in the near future. Exploration and experimentation in the field of spiritual science is ongoing and open-ended. In the next part of this epilogue I will give you detailed testimony from my own personal experiences and practical research over more than fifty years.

---

[16] Dr. David Fontana, Chartered Psychologist and Fellow of the British Psychological Society, is the author of twelve books. He has a special interest in exploring the results of paranormal research.

# Research Note

## Ectoplasm

Some readers who are not familiar with ectoplasm and materialisation may be wondering about these phenomena. Ectoplasm is a subtle living matter in the physical body, primarily invisible, but destroyed by light. It is capable of assuming vaporous liquid or solid states and properties. It is exuded usually in the dark from the pores and the various orifices of the body, and is slightly luminous, the more so when condensed. The temperature of the room is usually lowered when ectoplasm is produced; it possesses a characteristic smell and is cold to the touch. This substance is held to be responsible for the production of all phenomena classed as 'physical', and is the substance out of which materialized forms are built by the spirit operators. In addition they build elastic or rigid rods to produce movement in objects (telekinesis), raps and noises; artificial 'voiceboxes' for the phenomena of the direct and independent voice. The levitation of tables and heavy objects is accomplished by building extensible columns under them. Hands have materialized. Solid balls of cold light are familiar manifestations in physical phenomena.

Ectoplasm has been photographed on many occasions and appears opaque white, by infra-red flashlight which is the usual method employed. Sudden exposure to white light is of great physical danger to the medium when the ectoplasm is being used, due it seems, to its swift elastic recoil as it returns to its source. Hence a red light is used to avoid the danger and destruction of the material. In movement it can be swift or slow, it can build a perfect representation of a living human body with pulse warmth and muscular movement. Dr Dombrowski of the Polish S.P.R. had a sample analyzed in 1916 and to quote a summary of the bacteriological report: *"The substance is albuminoid matter, accompanied by fatty matter and cells found in the human organism. Starch and sugar, discoverable by Dr. Fehling's test, are absent."* [See Blunsdon (1963) p69]

Further verification of materialization is documented by Gustav Geley (1927, pp182–197) who did extensive research with well-known psychics Eva C., Madame Esperance, and Eusapio Paladino. Additionally Dr Dombrovski of the Polish SPR had ectoplasm analysed and his documentations showed a positive similar analysis of the substance in the human body.

## WITNESS TESTIMONY

### Synchronicity

In this second part of my case I will be the first witness, giving details of my search for evidence. Synchronicity has played an important part in my life, no more so than in my pursuit of evidence of the afterlife. By synchronicity I refer to the self-conscious movement of energy which motivates change and brings the projected vibrations into alignment. I have already made reference to Paul's Epistles in the Bible. He had spoken to the Corinthians about "diverse spiritual gifts given by the spirit of God, the Divine Power."[17] Since these gifts are very much in existence today I thought it fitting to use this premise as a working hypothesis. I began by searching for a teacher, a Guru, a medium, or psychic who would be reliable and trustworthy, and could assist me in my work.

### Lilian Bailey

I learnt of a psychic called Lilian Bailey who was contacted through my links with the *Psychic News*, London, England. Lilian Bailey had been the one-time medium psychic to the late Queen Mother and was a medium of some repute, respected by psychics and researchers alike. Her sittings with the Queen Mother have now been confirmed by Buckingham Palace[18].

My investigations started in the late 1950s with private sittings and weekly séances with Lilian Bailey, over a period of three years. Bill

---

[17] Corinthians 1, Ch.12. v. 1–12.
[18] *Psychic News* June 18th 2005 p7.

(Gordon) Adams, Manager of the Psychic News Bookshop, and two other trustworthy people were included in the group. The purpose of our séances with Lilian Bailey was to develop trance mediumship and to experience the materialization of spirit into visible form, using ectoplasm[19]. As our séances progressed we began to attain a heightened level of energy which eventually produced ectoplasm. We experienced the lifting of a huge mahogany table with luminous tabs for guidance in the dimly lit séance room. In addition, to enhance the vision of floating ectoplasmic rods, we used a 4"x3" piece of 3–ply wood, covered with luminous paint, which floated across the floor. These rods usually exuded from the séance team, from some more than others. In the course of time, a large aluminium trumpet shape (also daubed with luminous paint) was brought into use. This floated around and drifted across the room to the corners of a seven-foot high ceiling, emitting voices in several different languages which were unknown to the team. An exciting highlight came when the large trumpet opened in half in mid-air, whizzed around like a Catherine-wheel and then re-assembled itself gently on the floor.

Other instruments with appropriate music were brought into play, such as a pair of castanets and a luminous painted tambourine. These were extremely successful. At one séance, while in trance, Lilian Bailey had the spirit of a sun god, Rashin Ra[20] who came through to tell me he was my spirit mentor and guide. He also told me that I was on a special mission in this life to seek for truth. He still makes his presence known to me. All the séances were carefully guarded by a spirit called "Abdul". Bill Adams organised and ensured the continued use of music of various sorts – sing-songs were encouraged which helped to raise

---

[19] See earlier Research Note on ectoplasm.
[20] Lilian had also said that this sun god was from the time of Ptolemy the Second. I have found this to be a correct historical reference.

the energy vibrations within the group. These were exciting years of discovery and confirmation. I had learned so much about physical mediumship through personal participation.

After three years Lilian felt that enough had been achieved in our séances and urged me to move on in search of other mediums/psychics of expertise. I went to several presentations which included materialisations. One such presentation was at a large meeting attended by over one hundred people who had come to see the work of the renowned psychic Alec Harris, from Wales. At this meeting there were over nine materialisations. One of these was my grandmother who made her presence known to me under a dim red light. In awe of what I was witnessing, I was at first uncertain of her identity because she appeared much younger than I remembered her and the image was hazy, but after a few moments I could distinguish her features in the dim light and after asking a barrage of questions to verify her identity, I was satisfied that indeed this was my grandmother. I asked Gran if she would depart with love and disappear in my presence, and not drift away behind the drapes, as is usually done. Gran, who had nursed me from an early age, replied that I would not like it. I told her that it would help me in my research. She then appeared to "melt" away like a candle from her head down to her feet. I was able to see the ectoplasm flowing back behind the drapes into the body of the medium, Alec Harris, who was visible to me through the drapes. This profound experience convinced me of the reality of spirit communication through the medium of materialisation.

## Canada

Synchronicity also played its part in shaping my first meeting with Muriel, who was to become my wife. We were introduced through a mutual friend who was a healer at the Marylebone Spiritualist Association in London, England. She was a singer and I was an actor, but we also shared an interest in all things pertaining to the metaphysical. In 1960 I accompanied Muriel and her friend, Tricia, on a family visit to Aberdeen in Scotland. During our stay we met a well-respected Scottish medium, Edith Bruce who was giving an address and demonstration of clairvoyance at a church hall meeting. Edith Bruce announced that my Sioux Indian guide had told her that I would move to Toronto, Canada: *"You are on a mission with your research work and you will be helped"*. I found this hard to believe. At that point I could think of no reason why I might want to move to Canada. I married Muriel in 1963 and the service was followed by a small confirmation ceremony at the Marylebone Spiritualists Association, conducted by medium Ivy Northage (1909–2002).

Eventually in 1979, after a series of life-changing events unfolded, we emigrated from the UK to Canada. So here we were in Toronto almost twenty years later just as Edith had predicted but there was a sequel to this. Unbeknown to us Edith had also moved to Toronto only a few months earlier. A short time after, through pure synchronistic alignment (there is no such thing as chance) we met up with her once again. So not even Edith suspected that her prediction of twenty years ago would also include her! This was the beginning of a long and fruitful friendship.

**Edith Bruce**

Edith had gained recognition for her spiritual healing work and was ordained as a minister. Reverend Edith Bruce worked tirelessly to help people cope with their sickness and stress, guiding them back to stability through her constant healing ministry. Her work seemed fitting to be remembered in a more permanent way. We considered a book on her life, but I did not have the time to devote to such a project. Although her own book, *'The Keys to the Kingdom'*, was shortly to be published (1997), this still did not seem to me to guarantee longevity and I had to give the matter further thought.

During my research into the work of William James, I was struck by a passage in his book *'The Will to Believe'* (1956) which told of the Ingersoll Lectureship at Harvard University in the USA. This was the inspiration which led me to the task of initiating a similar event in our home University, the University of Toronto. After some lengthy negotiations to convince the Philosophy Department of the ongoing positive interest in matters of a metaphysical nature, we eventually achieved the desired result of an annual Edith Bruce lectureship on 'Life After Death' established for posterity in 1996. These annual lectures have since been transferred to the Department of Religious Studies at the University of Toronto, emulating the annual Ingersoll Lectureship at Harvard University. Reverend Edith Bruce has since retired her active role in mediumship and I am sure that her work will be rewarded in spirit.

## Ian Currie as Witness

Here we come to another important meeting which had a significant effect on our lives. Muriel and I were watching TV one evening, when we heard Ian Currie speaking on reincarnation and afterlife. I felt strongly that we should meet with this Professor and arranged to have lunch with him. During our lunch meeting Muriel gave him a very accurate psychic reading which impressed him greatly. Ian and I soon struck up a good relationship that continued for many years. I joined the

Association for Past Life Experiences, to which Ian already belonged, together with a group of other professors, including the reputable Professor Adam Crabtree, who still remains a good friend. We gave many lectures on our research through this Association.

Ian Currie was known to many across North America through his work on radio and television and of course his book *'You Cannot Die'*. He was an exponent and practitioner in past life regression, indeed he was acknowledged to be one of the foremost authorities on past lives regression and paranormal research. During our time together he made a pact with me that whoever passed on first, would attempt to come to the other through a psychic or a medium. As you are aware Ian kept his promise by appearing to Muriel a month after his passing, and subsequently was able to answer many of my direct questions about the spirit world in his one hundred or so conversations with Muriel. He provided us with his positive evidence of life in the spirit world and the survival of intelligence. It was wonderful for me to hear from Muriel his first few words when referring to the afterlife: "Tell Bill the good news is: There is one – **Life continues**".

## Muriel as Witness

You will already be aware of the psychic gifts of my dear wife Muriel. By the time we arrived in Canada she was already well established in clairvoyance, clairaudience and clairsentience. Hunt (1996) states that medium/psychics have a frequency of 400 – 200,000 energy cycles per second. I was told that with Muriel's qualities she would rank somewhere high in the latter frequency, enabling her to reach the higher realms of consciousness in the ethereal world; this would make her spiritual observations of great value to me in my ongoing research.

Muriel's detailed conversations with Ian Currie are, of course, the major subject of this book. The accurate handwritten recordings have been demonstrated earlier. Additionally she continued to provide witness testimony of the survival of intelligence and the existence of life after death. She continued throughout her life to provide readings to many people, friends and family alike, helping them with their lives, careers, and business proposals. One such meeting involved M. Dale Palmer and his daughter Rosemary, at our Warlock Crescent home in November 2001.

Dale Palmer, of Indiana USA is a former District Attorney and successful lawyer in his own right. He is a passionate amateur historian who has spent over thirty years researching Western civilisation and its origins and religious doctrines in Egypt. A detailed account of Dale Palmer's research can be found in his (1994) book: *True Esoteric Traditions*.

In the meeting at our home on November 1st, 2000, Dale had been taping Muriel's clairvoyance and clairsentience capabilities for a couple of hours. At the end of the evening he felt the meeting had been very successful, so he asked her to request her guide, Chung, to try to find out what would be the results of the forthcoming American Presidential elections between George Bush and Al Gore. Muriel had never attempted this kind of prediction, and she knew little or nothing about American politics – nevertheless she agreed to give it a try. She later returned saying that she was confused and could not get a clear answer – first it was Gore, then Bush, and so it went back and forth. Dale encouraged her to consult further with Chung and so, after this second consultation she came back to Dale and said: "I am told that there is much confusion in American politics between these two men – but Bush will get it." Later when the results were announced the reader will know that Bush was elected after several recounts. However after the final result had been declared Dale Palmer phoned Muriel and told her: "How accurate and right you were – you said Bush would *get* it, not win it".

As a result of our meetings with Dale, Muriel and I were selected to be on the team of investigators for a private international Conference of the *Noetic Institute* in Plainville, Indiana, USA, in July 2001. The theme of this Conference was "Higher Reality and Electronic Voice Phenomenon (EVP)" and it was headed by Dale and Kay Palmer, together with Prof Gary Schwartz[21], Director of the Laboratory at the University of Arizona, Prof Euvaldo Cabral Jr, University of Sao Paulo, Sarah Estep, Ruth Mattson Taylor, Tom and Alisa Butler, Alex McRae, Isle of Skye, Scotland, and others of international importance. Muriel, Tricia and I witnessed a great volume of evidence on the survival of human intelligence. However Muriel's testimony as an accurate witness was also enhanced by the many private consultations she gave to participants at the Conference. Further evidence of Muriel's mediumship can be verified in her (2000) communication: *The Origin of the Scole Experiment* which was achieved through spirit communication.

The following year, 2002, Muriel and I were asked to make presentations at the Annual Conference of the Academy of Religion and Psychical Research (ARPR). This was Muriel's first public lecture, and sadly it was to be her only one. Her presentation is reproduced in Appendix I of this book and is a wonderful testimony of the development of her psychic awareness and of her mediumship during her lifetime. My dear wife has been a truly great witness in providing evidence of spiritual gifts and of the survival of human intelligence.

[21] See Schwartz and Russek (1999).

## Near-Death Experience

I have already recounted the evidence on near-death experiences however I have had my own personal experience of direct spirit communication, where a timely warning by a recently deceased friend helped to prevent my own death! I was alone in the house working on my computer. I started to feel weak and ill – I could not think – everything became fuzzy and I was on the point of passing out, but at that moment I heard my late friend's voice urging me to get out of the house immediately. By this time I was unable to stand but sensing the urgency somehow managed to drag myself to the front door. Once outside I began to feel better, still not knowing why I needed to leave but on going into the garage discovered there was a carbon monoxide leakage from the garage to the house – I had left the car running for several hours and without that timely warning I would surely have left this planet before my time! Thank you Gerald, my dear friend!

## Other Important Research and Developments

I have referred earlier to the writings of Dr Edgar Mitchell, the sixth moon astronaut, about consciousness. After he returned to earth he formed the International Institute of Noetic Sciences (IONS) in 1972. I was a regular participant at his conferences in the USA, and Edgar Mitchell also favoured me with the task of organising a Toronto membership for IONS. Similarly, I later became the Canadian liaison representative for the *Spiritual Scientist* Magazine which had developed from the Scole Group. Sadly this magazine is no longer being published.

## THE CONVERSATIONS

The conversations that took place between Muriel Williams and Ian Currie in the chapters of this book provide ample evidence of life in the spirit world and of spiritual gifts. One cannot help but notice Ian's humour (and that of Muriel) within the conversations. As Ian became more comfortable and honed his communication skills his personality and humour became an integral part of his conversations, many times Muriel would come upstairs laughing heartily at some of their exchanges during the session. Ian brought us many insights into life in spirit, but throughout the book he reiterated the importance of keeping a good perspective and balance in one's own life and continuing to seek for one's own truth. Ian also reminded us that he gave us his perspective of spirit life from his standpoint – as he saw things – and that his reality might differ from that of another. I guess this is also part of the illusion we call Life – everything is open to interpretation. I trust that this book may have shed a little more light in dark corners and was worthy of your interest and attention.

## CONCLUSION

I have presented you with witness testimony from my own research over my lifetime. I have not merely studied this subject but also actively explored, experienced, participated and witnessed all the different forms of phenomena, appertaining to spiritual science. It is fitting for exploration of the Afterlife to be acknowledged as Psychic Science or Metaphysical Science within the field of Physics. Indeed the term 'metaphysics' is now used for paranormal studies. The late Dr Kit Pedler, from England, well known in the field of Physics declared in a TV programme: *"It won't be long before all the tag words used by Scientists will cease to exist and be absorbed into the normal."* He believed that the words paranormal – supernormal – mystics – occult – psychics – need to be removed as they are words used by mainstream scientists today: human beings do not deserve these labels. English scientist, Rupert Sheldrake (1995) wrote: *"Human psychic powers begin to look more natural and biological than supernatural; when seen in the light of animal behaviour akin to the human sixth sense, we know for sure animals have"*.

These psychic gifts are bestowed on mankind for progressive knowledge of the soul, seeking eternal perfection. There has been a steady growth in spiritual awareness and spirituality in the minds of people today. The time is now right for more open development, more study, and a broader acknowledgment of this growing phenomenon.

### A Second Symposium

It is now almost 80 years since the SPR's (1926) public symposium on psychical belief was held. I feel strongly that the time has come to seriously consider a Second Symposium with the focus on: 'Survival of

Human Intelligence and Personality after Death'. There are many excellent researchers in this field who could be invited to make presentations. There is an abundance of evidential material and new scientific data that has become available since that first Symposium. A second Symposium with a working hypothesis involving all aspects of spiritual science is required to prove that life exists after death.

## Summation

Finally, putting this epilogue into a nutshell, I have stated my case for the 'Positive Survival of Human Personality'. We are primarily spiritual beings in a material body, we return home to the spiritual domain after death. **We always retain our free will, our personality, and our memory.** This is a crucial statement and one that needs time for reflection.

I have put my case before you. I have presented evidence that has been documented and authenticated over thousands of years. I have also provided you with my own witness testimony and the evidence of the conversations between Muriel and Ian which are contained in this book. For me, the case for survival of human personality after death has been irrefutably made. But you are the Judge and the Jury now – the choice is yours. I have truly enjoyed sharing this knowledge with you. *The good news is – life continues after death.*

Further information can be found on my web-site
www.evidencefromthespiritworld.com

Bill O.C. Williams, Ph.D.

# Bibliographic References

The following works are the specific references to publications and authors found in this book. Bill Williams has a vast library of books and periodicals covering many subjects relevant to the study of psychic phenomena. The books in his collection have contributed to his lifelong research and his immeasurable knowledge of psychic phenomena.

Alsop, Samuel C R (1989): *Whispers of Immortality*, Regency Press.

Archer, Fred (1966): *Exploring the Psychic World*, William Morrow & Co., NY.

Bailey, Alice (1993): *Esoteric Healing*, Lucis Publishing Co., NY.

Barrett, Richard (1995): *A Guide to Liberating the Soul*, Fulfilling Books, Virginia.

Blunsdon, Norman (1963): *Spiritualism (A popular dictionary of)*, Citadel Press.

Brown, Rosemary (1971): *Unfinished Symphonies: Voices from Beyond*, William Morrow & Co.

Bruce, Edith (1997): *Keys to the Kingdom*, Light Technology Publishing, Arizona.

Burr, Harold Saxton and Northrop, F.S.C. (1935): 'The Electro-dynamic Theory of Life' in *Quarterly Review of Biology* Vol. 10, pp322–333.

Borgia, Anthony (1954): *Life in the World Unseen*, published 1970, Corgi Books.

Cerutti, Edwina (1977): *Mystic with Healing Hands: The Life Story of Olga Worrell*, Harper & Row, San Francisco.

Colombo, John (undated): *The Ghost of Mackenzie King*, Hounslow Press.

Crabtree, Adam (1997): *Trance Zero*, Somerville House Publishing, Toronto.

Cummins, Geraldine (1925): *The Road to Immortality*, Psychic Press Ltd., London, UK.

Currie, Ian (1978): *You Cannot Die – the Incredible Findings of a Century of Research on Death*, Methuen Books.

Edwards, John (1998): *One Last Time*, Berkley Books.

Fisher, Joe (1990): *Hungry Ghosts*, Doubleday Canada Ltd., Toronto.

Flammarion, Camille (1924): *Haunted Houses*, T Fisher Unwin Ltd. London, UK.

Fontana, David (1992): Electronic Voice Phenomena Revisited, *Light Magazine*, Winter, pp100-105, College of Psychic Studies, London, UK.

Foy, Robin (1996): *In Pursuit of Physical Mediumship*, Janus Publishing Co.

Geley, Gustav (1927): *Clairvoyance and Materialisation*, George Doran & Co.

Hunt, Valerie (1996): *Infinite Mind: Science of the Human Vibrations of Consciousness*, Malibu Publishing Co, Cal. USA.

James, William (1956): *The Will to Believe / Human Immortality*, Dover Pub, NY.

—— (1960): *The Varieties of Religious Experience – A Study in Human Nature*, Fontana/Collins.

Kardec, Allen (1972): *The Spirits' Book*. (Translated by Anna Blackwell from the original 1857 work.) Lake-Livraria Allan Kardec Editora Ltda, Brasil.

Kubis, P and Macey, M (1997): *Conversations Beyond the Light*, Griffin Publishing.

Kubler Ross, Elizabeth (1974): *Death and Dying*, Macmillan Publishing Co., NY.

Ledair, Robert C (1966) (ed): The *Letters of William James and Theodore Flournoy*, Univ. of Wisconsin Press, USA.

Mattson Taylor, Ruth (1975): *Witness from Beyond*, Foreward Books.

—— (1999): *Evidence from Beyond*, Brett Books Inc.

Mayer, Gladys (1956): *Color and Healing* and *Man's Threefold Nature in* 'Color Healing' – A Survey compiled by Health Research, California.

Mitchell, Dr Edgar with Williams, Dwight (1966): *The Way of the Explorer*, Putnam & Sons.

Moody, Raymond (1975): *Life after Life*, Mocking Bird Books.

Murchison Carl (1927) (Ed): *The Case For and Against Psychical Belief*, Clark University, Massachusetts, USA.

Murphy, Gardner and Ballou, Robert O (1960): *William James on Psychical Research*, Viking Press, New York.

Nearing, Helen (1998): *Light on Aging*, Harcourt Brace & Co.

Osis, Karlis and Haraldsson, Erlendur (1977): *At the Hour of Death*, Avon Books, NY.

Osborne Leonard, Lady Gladys (1931): *My Life in Two Worlds*, Cassell.

—— (1937): *The Last Crossing*, Cassell.

—— (1942): *Brief Darkness*, Cassell.

Palmer, Dale (1994): *True Esoteric Traditions*, Noetics Institute.

Raudive, Konstantine (1971): *Breakthrough*, Colin Smythe.

Ring, Kenneth (1984): *Healing Towards Omega*, Morrow (1998): *Life at Death*, Conrad McCann.

Roberts, Jane (1970): *The Seth Material*, Prentice Hall.

Rogo, D Scott (1977): *Man does Survive Death*, Citadel Press Secaucus, NJ.

Schwatz, Gary and Russek, Linda (1999): *The Living Energy Universe*, Hampton Roads Publishing Co.

Sheldrake, Rupert (1995): *Seven Experiments that Could Change the World*, Riverhead Books.

—— (1996): Presentation at the Institute of Noetic Sciences Conference.

Smith, Raymond (1995): *Nobody Wants to Listen – and Yet!* CON-PSY Publications, Middlesex, UK.

Smythe, Frank and Stemman, Roy (1991): *Mysteries of the Afterlife*, Bloomsbury Books.

Solomon, Grant and Jane (1999): *The Scole Experiment*, Piatkus Publishers, London.

Stead, WT and Woodman, Pardoe (c1922): *The Blue Island: Experiences of a New Arrival Beyond the Veil*, The Austin Publishing Company of California.

St-Pierre, Catherine (1994): *Thou Art Peter*, Editions Magnificat, Canada.

Sugrue, Thomas (1942): *There is a River*, Henry Holland & Co, USA.

Tart, Charles (1997): *Body Mind Spirit – Exploring the Parapsychology of Spirituality*, Hampton Roads Publishing Co.

Toksvic, Signe (1948): *Emanuel Swedenburg*, Yale University Press, New Haven.

Van Praagh, James (1997): *Talking to Heaven*, Penguin Group USA.

Williams, Bill (2002): Survival of Human Intelligence and Personality after Death, *Proc of the Academy of Religion and Psychical Research (ARPR) Annual Conference*, 2002 pp69-78.

Williams, Muriel (2000): Origin of the Scole Experiment, *The Spiritual Scientist*, Winter Vol. 3, No. 1 pp10-11.

—— (2002): Mediumship, *Proc of the Academy of Religion and Psychical Research (ARPR) Annual Conference*, 2002 pp79-83.

## Appendix I

# An Autobiographical Account of the Mediumship of Muriel Williams

### THE ACADEMY OF RELIGION AND PSYCHICAL RESEARCH

MEDIUMSHIP: A GATEWAY TO OTHER DIMENSIONS OF EXISTENCE

**PROCEEDINGS** of Annual Conference 2002

---

**MEDIUMSHIP**

**Muriel Williams**

---

*As a medium, it has been my privilege to be able to communicate with spirit. Over a period of about seven years, I have had conversations with the spirit of the late Professor Ian Currie. He has consistently communicated his findings, and talked about his life in spirit since his passing in 1992. In this presentation I discuss my work and how I communicate with spirit, and relate examples of these communications.*

The ability to communicate directly with spirit is indeed a gift. Those of us who share this gift, I'm sure would agree it is a privilege to be able to bridge the gap between the two worlds. Before discussing my mediumship I would like to tell you about some of the events in my life, which helped to advance my psychic awareness, and bring me into focus.

I was born in Aberdeen Scotland and grew up on a small farm just outside the city. When I was about 12 years old, working in the fields I would see visions and hear voices. As I grew older, I realized that many of the pictures I'd seen as a child were premonitions of my own future.

In my late teens I was fortunate to meet an excellent medium, her name was Jean Rollo. She took me to spiritual meetings and encouraged me to participate, which helped to develop my clairvoyance. Jean also had a healing circle. I'm not a healer, but I remember sitting in that circle watching the streams of blue light coming from the fingers of the healers, apparently I was the only one present who could actually see the energy. This really impressed me and I realized there was a force, which I could connect with.

I moved to London in my twenties to further my career as a professional singer and dancer. During this period I was led to a spiritual source in Belgrave Square, The Spiritualist Association of Great Britain, of which I am still a member. Back then it was known as The Marylebone Spiritualist Association (M.S.A.).

I spent many wonderful hours there. You could listen to great mediums like Ivy Northage and Estelle Roberts. I met Harry Edwards, the founder of the Spiritual Healing Foundation. However, the most exciting thing for me was being invited to join a developing circle headed by Stanley Poulton, a well-known medium at the Association. I learned so much, while sitting in that circle. The most valuable lesson was when Stanley's guide Chang focused his attention on me and said ... "you are withholding information – you are here to develop your psychic gift – you must share what you are seeing and hearing – and most important – TRUST YOUR GUIDE – TRUST YOUR CHANNEL. You are not the judge of the information you receive. What might appear to be nonsense to you, could be wonderful proof to the person it is intended for." From that time forward I have never doubted my guide Master Chung, and always given out without question.

Of course the most influential happening in my life, was meeting my husband Bill. This came about through a healer friend who was part of the M.S.A. healing group she arranged for Bill and I to meet. He was an actor and I a singer and we shared a common interest in the field of the paranormal. So here we are, 50 years later, which brings me to the point of this presentation.

**Mediumship – and how I communicate with the spirit world.**

I am clairvoyant, clairaudient and clairsentient. I am not comfortable with the trance state. I prefer to be fully aware when I am communicating, much like having a telephone conversation. I hear the words and write them down, or communicate them verbally. Our book, *'Hi There I'm over Here, My Life in the Spirit World.'*[1] is the result of years of communication with the spirit of the late Professor Ian Currie. The purpose of the book is to give readers an insight into the workings of the spirit world, his life, personal experiences and findings, and of course to bring proof of the afterlife, which he presents in a clear, concise manner.

All this came about through Bill's friendship with the Professor. They were both members of the Past Lives Association. I got to know him when he needed some help from spirit, we had several sittings together. Sadly Ian passed over in July '92. So when he made his first contact with me from the spirit world, I was delighted but somewhat unprepared.

[1] This was the working title for the book.

I was sitting in the subway train on my way to business. I had drifted into a little meditation when Chung suddenly presented himself. He intimated that someone was standing by and wanted to talk to me, I gave the okay and immediately the figure of the late Prof. Ian Currie appeared in front of me. To say I was surprised would be an understatement, he gave a little smile as much as to say yes it is me, and then indicated that he wanted me to write something down. I found some scribble paper in my bag and started to write his message, it was quite brief, which was just as well because I was fast approaching my station and had to quickly exit the train. The purpose of the message was just to say, "hello I'm here, I want to communicate with you. Tell Bill if he's still wondering if there's an afterlife the good news is – there is."

Now you may be wondering why Ian chose such an unlikely place to make his first contact, well the answer is really quite simple – opportunity – it was my quiet state of mind that opened up the line of communication, the location was totally irrelevant. At this time I was heavily involved in our business, finding time for meditation and communication with spirit was almost impossible, so I would grab 15 minutes while traveling. This day, Ian seized the moment in order to make his presence known to me. This was the beginning of a long association. We arranged definite times for our communications, which I had to fit into my busy schedule.

Until the Professor came along I'd never written on a continuous basis, nor kept in constant communication with one spirit being other than my own guide. I have always given readings and on occasions would write a letter from a loved one in spirit wishing to communicate with their family. However this was a much bigger undertaking and a new experience for me, which was quite exciting. We shared about 106 communications, apart from the times when he would come around, make his presence known and comment on something topical or share some other information. Ian became almost like one of the family, he was so familiar to us.

At this point I should explain how I prepare to communicate with spirit. Because of the exacting nature of the communications with Ian, it was necessary to assure myself that I was working within the stream of intelligence. I had to raise my energy frequency into a higher level of awareness to ensure as clear a line as possible during the communication. I would go into a short meditation focusing into the centre of the forehead, which is the middle eye or third eye as it is sometimes called; then start to expand my energy field until Master Chung came into focus. He would tell me that my channel to the spirit world was open and ready for me to communicate. Master Chung guards my channel at all times and vets, whoever wishes to come through. Ian has often remarked, "You need a pass card to get by him!"

When I am ready to communicate with Ian I sense his presence, then see him clearly in front of me. I can describe what he's wearing and sense his mood. At this point, I am aware that I have reached the level of thought in my consciousness that will allow me to connect with, and transmit his thoughts. That is how I make my connection to Ian.

Now, I was curious to find out how Ian makes his connection to me, so I asked him about this, and he said. "It is extremely interesting how the circuit works between us. You are like a switchboard, which I plug into once I have the okay from Chung. I recognize your signal, which is a turquoise light attached to your aura and spirit battery. Once I have made the contact with you, our frequencies come into line and resonate with each other, then we're in business!"

Once I became familiar with Ian's distinctive energy it was easy for me to pick up his vibration. In a way it's the same as recognizing a signature or knowing a familiar voice on the telephone, I could send out a signal to him and vice versa. Over time Ian and I were able to perfect our channel, he called it the hot line! It became possible to maintain a clear line of communication for longer periods of time, on the other hand we also learned what would cause weaknesses in the link and be able to detect changes in the level of the energy frequency. We need to remember that this form of communication is not an exact science, and the level of success is governed by certain conditions.

I believe it is possible that cosmic disturbances around our planet can interfere with the quality of the communication, almost like static on a radio frequency can interfere with transmission. Also, if I did not feel too well my energy would be low, or if Ian happened to be in low spirits and below par, then our energies would not resonate, and the line would break up. This happened on more than one occasion. There is one other important point to mention here, and that is, getting out of the way of the communication. Occasionally I would start thinking about what I was writing, instead of keeping the line clear for the incoming thoughts that Ian was projecting. Of course the flow was immediately interrupted. Ian always knew when this was happening and I would hear him say "just write, don't think!" and then he would wait for me to get back on track. So that was the bad news now here is the good news.

There were times when my energy field would expand dramatically, and I was able to reach the frequency required to gain access into the spirit world. At this level I could see into the realms of spirit and be consciously present in the ethereal surroundings. At other times, I witnessed scenes of special celebration in the spirit world; what I cannot confirm is whether the ceremony was taking place at that moment, or whether I was viewing a past or future event. However there were a number of times during communication with Ian when I again experienced this altered state. On one occasion I was privileged to witness an inauguration scene, which was unbelievable, and dare I say, "out of this world." The colours of the spirit robes outshone our most spectacular screen epic.

At another time when I made contact with Ian, we had this interesting conversation on the use of energy in the spirit world. This came about because I noticed a change in the energy around him, it was lighter and he appeared to be encased in an aura, like a flimsy sort of tent. I saw and sensed the presence of other spirit personalities in his vicinity; I asked him about this and he replied.

"You have described the energy surrounding us, which is like a huge cobwebby cloak, I say us, because I have brought a student group with me. We are in the light because of our collective energy, your spiritual eye is quite accurate." He continues, "when I plan to have a get-together or class, I send out thoughts so other fellow spirit beings will pick up the vibration, and be on the energy line for my message. I pinpoint an area, indicating a circle, and then a small radius of energy starting from me, will link up with whoever plans to attend. When these energies link up, they create a powerhouse or centre, which surrounds us with energy and protection, which means that communication is hooked up. So what you called a 'tent' is actually the combined energy vibration, which creates a temporary room for our discussion." Ian finished off by saying, "It's all clever stuff, and it happens in a flash!" I thought this was fascinating. It's like a sort of spiritual auditorium, with a built in communication system.

Ian went on to say that the system of communication within the spirit world is the same whether it is a meeting between individuals, a teaching seminar, a family gathering or a grand ceremonial occasion. The energy is used in exactly the same way. It is the natural law of the Universe. In our physical world, the energy has been transformed into matter. We build meeting places for the same purposes, and communicate with each other through channels of energy; there is absolutely no difference. The ethereal world is a wonderful organized system of divine law.

I would like to end by relating an incident of how a young man from spirit quickly latched on to my wave length, in order to set up a line of communication. On this morning, Bill was in his office talking on the phone. I passed his open door en route to the laundry room. As I walked in, a young man 'appeared' in front of me. In surprise I said, "can I help you, why are you here?" As I tuned in to his vibration I sensed that he was angry and frustrated. He kept repeating, "I shouldn't be here – I shouldn't be here, it's not my time." I asked him again, "Why have you come to me?" His reply was clear. "You will know when your husband finishes his call."

When Bill had completed his call, I asked whom he had been talking to. He said it was an associate, who had just lost his only son quite suddenly, in his early forties. Well, there was no doubt in my mind that the vision I had just seen was indeed his son, and the young man expressed a great desire to speak with his father. Bill called his friend back and arranged for me to talk with him, and mediate for his son in spirit. I can tell you it was a profound experience. The father was able to identify his son without question because of the proof that was given. We had a number of telephone communications, and I also wrote some letters to the father from his son.

We should understand that arriving on the other side does not necessarily mean that we are now at peace, and happy loving souls. This still young man, was taken through a very short, freak illness just as he was preparing for election, and felt cheated out of life. It took him a long time to come to terms with this situation, but finally he was able to let go, and accept all the love and beauty that surrounded him in the spirit world.

I'd like to leave you with these words from my mentor Master Chung.

*We live in two beautiful worlds; but it is always your choice to use this understanding to benefit your soul, as it continues to grow and learn in the light of Immortality.*

*Blessings to your world.*

Born Muriel Mary McDonald Davidson in Aberdeen Scotland 1926. A tripartite medium. Clairvoyant, clairaudient, clairsentient, and psychic from early years. I followed a career in the performing Arts as a professional singer and dancer in London England. During this period, I studied mediumship at the Spiritualist Association of Great Britain, and still remain a member of that association.

My husband Bill and I immigrated to Toronto Canada in 1979 and I continue to give spiritual guidance to those in need. Co-author of the book: *'Hi There I'm Over Here – My Life in the Spirit World'* which was communicated by the spirit of the late Prof: Ian Currie. To be published – Fall 2002.[2]

---

[2] Unfortunately it was in the summer of 2002 that Muriel's health began to deteriorate and the draft manuscript lay dormant for two years.

# Appendix II

# A Sample of Muriel's Handwritten Notes of the Conversations

Saturday 29th @ 5-30pm. in the sanctuary

Mysteries of the mind are concealed in past lives + so your previous lives relate to the the present one. It varies quite a lot from one person to another because it depends on their spiritual advancement & progress they have made in their lives, it seems to be inevitable to show exactly what makes up the unseen mysteries of the mind but it most certainly all lies with the past. Of cause how one is conducting their present life, is also important to knowing where the hidden thoughts lie. People would find life easier if they could understand lots of the inner lines

Handwriting samples have been reduced to 65% of original size to fit on these pages.

thoughts — where they come from. Creative minds & talented beings usually find, that they have since children, wanted to be — in the line they are — because they have been directed into their present path from a previous existence. One could elaborate more into this part of the Psychic but I will leave off & look forward tonight to talking with you.

My energy-vib. is a little weak now so I'll shut off till later ——— I may have a surprise for you — don't know if I can Link-it up.

Ian

# Index

Afterlife, 1, 2, 3, 6, 10, 14, 17, 18, 19, 22, 25, 54, 86, 101, 107, 128, 135, 155, 156, 172, 174, 178, 179, 184
Akashic records, 139, 141
Angels, 61
Aura, 21, 22, 43, 45, 46, 47
Baby, See children
Bailey, Lilian, 174-5
Bible, 7, 139, 157, 158, 159, 161-2
Blue Island, 123-4
Blue Planet, 121-4
Bruce, Edith, 177,178
Children, 73, 75, 76, 118
Christmas, 133-4
Chung, 1, 2, 3, 9-10, 38, 43, 45, 87, 144-5, 149, 180
Colour, 9, 11, 18, 20, 21, 22, 29, 54, 59, 60, 86, 100, 124
Conception, 73, 123
Consciousness, 51, 52, 74, 104, 107, 108, 109, 139, 143, 145, 151, 157, 159-60
Crabtree, Adam, 121, 149, 179
Crookes, William, 164, 165
DNA, 71, 72, 76, 143
Dreams, 108, 109

Easter, 95, 96
Ectoplasm, 81, 165, 173, 175-6
Energy, 1, 18, 20, 22, 24, 28, 29, 31, 37-48, 55, 64, 73, 74, 76, 77, 78, 81, 82, 85, 87, 88-9, 97, 100, 104, 112, 118, 120, 121, 130, 132, 151, 157, 160, 174-6, 179
Euthanasia, 95, 98, 101
Exorcism, 119
Fate, 131
Fisher, Joe, 93
Flying, 103, 104, 105
Free Will, 5, 17, 44, 61, 85, 90, 97, 98, 128, 132, 134, 135, 138, 141, 148, 150, 185
Freedom of choice, 52, 96
Friendship, 27
Gandhi, 63
Guides, 59, 61-5, 71, 93
Healers, 22, 64
Higher levels, 114, 129, 134, 137, 151, 152
Higher planes, 28, 66, 114, 128, 138
Incarnation, 32, 33, 49, 61, 62, 75, 78, 111, 112 (also see reincarnation)
James, William, 164, 178
Joan of Arc, 162
Judgement scene, 12

King, Mackenzie, 167
King, Martin Luther, 63
Lectures, 17, 19, 27, 28, 29, 31-3, 66, 67, 84
Levels, 21, 27, 34, 50, 55, 66, 77, 81, 82, 85, 89, 134, 137-42, 144
Light, 11, 22, 27, 40, 43, 45, 46, 54, 72, 80, 90, 126, 142, 152, 156, 173
Lincoln, Abraham, 167
Lodge, Oliver, 35, 165-6
Lower level, 27, 89, 138, 140-1, 145
Masters, 31, 59, 61, 65-66, 71, 79, 84, 128, 133, 138, 139, 150
Materialisation, 165, 170, 173, 176
Memory, 70, 71, 108, 113-4, 122, 146, 168, 185
Mental health/illness, 97, 115
Miscarriage, 76
Mother Theresa, 126
Mulki, Joseph, 60
Multiple personalities, 116-7, 119
Murder, 99
Music, 26, 141
Near-Death Experiences, 11, 80, 103, 106-7, 168
Out-of-body experiences, 103
Past life regression, See regression
Personality, 5, 23, 36, 50, 64, 71, 72, 76, 112, 114-5, 116, 117, 118, 119, 120, 143, 144, 155, 157, 158, 164
Pets, 77, 78, 79, 80
Poltergeists, 85-86, 88, 91
Possession, 118-9, 123
Rapport, 3, 4, 6
Regression, 17, 49, 70, 87, 105, 107, 113, 115, 118, 121, 179

Reincarnation, 21, 42, 50, 69-70, 76-77, 89, 93, 98, 112, 114, 178
Religion, 125-8, 130, 156, 158
Scole, 170-2, 181, 182
Sleep, 10, 11, 27, 41, 42, 103, 105, 106, 108, 109
Solomni, 65
Soul, 2, 3, 4, 18, 20, 21-4, 26, 27, 31, 32, 34, 36, 40, 41, 44, 46, 47, 49-56, 59, 60, 62, 63, 66, 69-76, 85, 86, 88-90, 96-7, 99, 100, 103-6, 111-2, 114-9, 123, 124, 126-30, 132, 135-6, 140-8, 166, 169
Soul progress, 142, 143, 144, 146
Spirit impostors, 85, 86, 93
Spiritual credits, 19, 31, 72, 144, 153
Spiritual growth, 21, 31, 40, 55, 76, 85, 135, 142
Spiritual laws, 21, 70, 73, 95, 96, 99, 114, 127, 158
Spiritual progress, 21, 29, 42, 51, 56, 70, 75, 95, 96, 98, 105, 127, 137, 138, 142
Suicide, 95, 96, 97, 98, 101
Swedenborg, 29, 35-6
Teaching, 49-51, 53, 70, 83, 89, 130, 137, 138, 142, 162-3
Tennis, 20, 23, 28, 32, 89, 150
Time, 4, 15, 18, 24, 26-8, 32, 38, 39, 51, 66, 70, 96, 106, 108
Transcendental meditation, 104
Travel, 20, 21, 27, 31-2, 98, 104-5, 147, 150
Turquoise light, 42, 43, 44-5, 46, 103
White light, 9, 11
Willpower, 20, 104

ISBN 155369098-2
9 781553 690986

Made in the USA